Inspiring | Educating | Creating | Entertaining

Brimming with creative inspiration, how-to projects, and useful information to enrich your everyday life, Quarto Knows is a favorite destination for those pursuing their interests and passions. Visit our site and dig deeper with our books into your area of interest: Quarto Creates, Quarto Cooks, Quarto Homes, Quarto Lives, Quarto Drives, Quarto Explores, Quarto Gifts, or Quarto Kids.

10 9 8 7 6 5 4 3 2 1

ISBN: 978-0-7603-5939-6

Library of Congress Cataloging-in-Publication Data

Names: McLaughlin, Chris, 1964- author. | Flynn, Nadeen, photographer.
Title: Growing heirloom flowers : bring the vintage beauty of heritage blooms to your modern garden / Chris McLaughlin ; photography by Nadeen Flynn.
Description: Minneapolis, MN : Cool Springs Press, 2018. | Includes index.
Identifiers: LCCN 2017049983 | ISBN 9780760359396 (plc)
Subjects: LCSH: Flower gardening. | Flowers--Heirloom varieties. | Heirloom varieties (Plants)
Classification: LCC SB405 .M415 2018 | DDC 635.9--dc23
LC record available at https://lccn.loc.gov/2017049983

Acquiring Editors: Madeleine Vasaly and Mark Johanson
Project Manager: Alyssa Bluhm
Art Director: Cindy Samargia Laun
Photographer: Nadeen Flynn
Cover Design, Page Design, and Illustrations: Evelin Kasikov

Printed in China

MIX
Paper from responsible sources
FSC® C101537

GROWING
HEIRLOOM
FLOWERS

Bring the Vintage Beauty of Heritage Blooms to Your Modern Garden

Chris McLaughlin

Photography by Nadeen Flynn

COOL
SPRINGS
PRESS

CONTENTS

INTRODUCTION

AN HEIRLOOM FLOWER REVIVAL

Fashion dictates everything. All it takes is one or two trendsetters to spot something that tickles their fancy—they parade it around publicly, and voilà! The rest of us are soon following suit, running around like goats in a spring rain.

Well, hallelujah, flower gardens have once again come into vogue and *heirlooms* are now celebrating their day in the sun! Not to worry about fleeting trends in this case. Flower gardening is just beginning to hit its stride, and the heirloom flower resurgence is in its infancy, headed for a long and healthy life.

We have Italy to thank for the "slow food" movement, and this undoubtedly paved the way for the "slow flower" movement. We, the people, are finally embracing local, sustainable, and quality *everything*. We're once again growing our own flowers for our own homes. It shouldn't come as any surprise that the matriarchs—the vintage flowers of our past—are calling to us.

As a huge flower fan, I truly appreciate cultivars of all kinds, even the brand-new, shiny varieties. But it's the club-of-plants-past that holds the flowers of my heart. This book is all about the *old-fashioned* flowers that connect yesterday's gardeners to today's gardeners and most assuredly to tomorrow's gardeners.

DEFINING HEIRLOOM FLOWERS

So, what exactly are heirloom flowers? The definition is either going to be exciting or frustrating, depending on your personality. If you're a control freak, this whole thing is going to give you a nervous tic. Fair warning. The truth is that there are no hard-and-fast rules when it comes to defining an heirloom plant—flower or otherwise. Rather, there are general guidelines that most garden enthusiasts agree are accepted heirloom definition(s).

A General Definition

Heirloom flowers have been enjoyed and cultivated by enthusiasts for hundreds and even thousands of years. Heirlooms are most often strictly defined as *open-pollinated* plants, which means that the plant flowers have been naturally pollinated by insects, birds, mammals, or the wind. Seeds produced by open pollination will produce future plants that look and perform ("breed true") like the parent plant. Heirlooms are a subset within the open-pollinated plant group. Open-pollinated plants earn the heirloom title if they have been cultivated and handed down through generations for 50 to 100 years.

All parts of *Echinacea* have been used as herbal medicine both historically and today.

Purists will say that the plant must be *at least* 100 years old to be considered an heirloom. Most enthusiasts, though, will say 50 years is sufficient, and still others use 1951 as a marker, because that's when seed companies began heavily marketing hybrid seed varieties. You can already see some definition wavering here. It's also worth mentioning that some of the "commercial" heirlooms that have been introduced more currently are often family heirlooms that a seed company purchased from the family and introduced to the general public.

Many heirlooms also come with an interesting backstory that's passed down as readily as the seeds. Although it isn't vital to have a story accompany them, the narratives are often surprising or enchanting, making heirlooms all the more charming.

An Additional Definition

There are ancient *hybrids* that are considered heirlooms in their own right. For example, old garden roses have a lovely array of varieties that were bred ages ago. These antiquities have been cherished and purposefully handed down through the generations to keep their legacy alive. In fact, most rose enthusiasts consider any cultivar that was bred before 1867 (when the first modern rose was introduced) to be an heirloom variety.

There are other species that have antique hybrids as well. I have a Japanese anemone in my garden, 'Honorine Jobert', which was introduced in 1858.

She's an heirloom if I've ever seen one. In my opinion, these beloved cultivars with antique heritage most certainly belong in the heirloom category. While most of the flowers in this book are open-pollinated plants, I have also added a few ancient heirloom-hybrids to the list.

No matter which definition a gardener subscribes to, an heirloom certainly is most aptly described as a cultivar that has been selected, raised, saved, and handed down generation after generation. Still, I can only imagine the heated debates over the garden gate have been epic. I'm going to leave it to you, dear reader, to define for yourself what is deemed an heirloom in your own garden. Personally, I think there are some compelling reasons to keep the term flexible. You might see it differently and to that I say, "*You* do *you*, my flower friend."

A note to my control-freaky gardeners: *Please don't obsess on this for too long. No matter which definition you choose, no one is going to take away your birthday.*

What Is a Hybrid Plant?

Hybrid plants are the resulting offspring of two different plant varieties. They're created to produce a desired trait, such as deeper color, larger blossoms (or fruit), or plant height. Hybrid varieties have a closely related gene pool, which leaves very little genetic diversity in the plant. What this means is that the seeds from a hybrid will not result in plants that look like their parent. They don't "breed true" and can look like any number of characteristics hidden inside its genetic code.

WE'RE ALL SMITTEN

One of the reasons gardeners are drawn to heirlooms is pure nostalgia. We humans are hardwired for it, and the warm fuzzy feeling that connects us to a garden belonging to a beloved grandparent or great-aunt makes a fine motivator. What better way to show our respect to these living antiques (the plants, that is) than to grow them near our own back porch and then pass our inheritance to the next generation of gardeners? Among all the perfectly sound reasons to grow heirlooms, this might honestly be the *best* reason. It's every bit as important to feed our hearts and souls as it is our stomachs and pocketbooks.

But wait, there's more! Try some amazing, heady scents. Naturally fragrant heirlooms are second to none in this category. Since the beginning of time, people have wanted to make themselves smell like flowers—so much so that we create chemical copycat versions and will pay a pretty penny for a knockoff of the real thing. Oh, my goodness, how we have sacrificed the fragrance of our flowers for other characteristics such as size, color, height, and longer-lasting blooms. Sure, some of these traits are quite nice . . . but the *fragrance*, y'all.

Heirlooms also happen to be notoriously easy-keepers in the garden. This feature alone is enough to make me a believer. Being old as the ages and routinely exposed to a bajillion climates, pests, and diseases makes one rather adaptable. Plants that pull their own to keep themselves alive in the garden are music to this gardener's ears.

Open-pollinated heirloom flowers bring with them a special gift—biological diversity. Biodiversity simply means "variety of life." It's important for the health of people and our ecosystems to keep as much natural genetic diversity in every species: plants, animals, people, and microorganisms. Grow open-pollinated heirlooms, save their seeds, replant, pass some along to another gardener, and you've earned a solid gold star!

One last thought about the pleasures of heirlooms. It's not always about the plants by themselves. It's the stories about how they came to grow in countries all over the world, stories about how they acquired their common names, stories of the famous people that painted them, stories about how your great-grandfather picked them for his true love every Sunday morning, and the story about how they ended up in *your* garden.

PLEASE PASS THEM ALONG

Heirlooms are also referred to as "passalong" plants. This term was coined by inspirational plantsman and garden writer Allen Lacy, and has since been revived by garden-writers-extraordinaire Steve Bender and Felder Rushing. Heirlooms are passalong plants because often the only way you're going to get your soil-grubby little hands on them is for a generous gardener to pass them along to you.

Lucky for us, gardeners *are* generous. It's one of our most endearing qualities (unless we're unloading zucchini on you). It's true that you may have a difficult time finding some vintage varieties at a nursery near you. However, even if you're the only person you know who digs in the dirt, no worries, as "ve have our vays"—our "vays" being through gardening friends and the seed companies listed in the back of this book.

To continue to see gorgeous blooms, rich fragrance, easy-keepers, history, compelling stories, and the genetic diversity of heirloom flowers in tomorrow's gardens, please feel free to pass them along.

Dahlias come in every color you can think of except blue.

Heirlooms depend on gardeners to pass them along.

1

BOLD BLOOMS FOR THE CUTTING GARDEN

*"A flowerless room is
a soulless room, to my way of thinking,
but even one solitary little vase of a
living flower may redeem it."*

—Vita Sackville-West

What's better than blooming heirloom flowers in your garden?
Blooming heirloom flowers in your house, of course!

———————————————————

I don't know anyone who doesn't love cutting armloads of bouquets from their own garden. Nothing replaces the fresh ambience that flowers bring to a room. While I would never discourage you from cutting any kind of flower for indoor arranging, there are some flowers especially suited for vase life because they tend to stay fresh the longest after being cut from the plant.

If you are like me, a little guilt might set in as you move through the garden, clipping stem after stem. It might feel as if you are stripping the garden of its beauty. But don't let your emotions get in the way of a gorgeous heirloom flower bouquet that costs only pennies. Remember that you are growing cutting flowers specifically to feed your soul, and you need to bring them indoors too, so you can be fed all day long. And remember that for many species, flower clipping encourages the plant to produce replacement blossoms. That's right, more flowers! So, harvest heirlooms for the house, leave a handful or two on the plants, and enjoy!

DAHLIA

(*DAHLIA* SPP.)

Dahlia was named for the Swedish botanist, Andreas Dahl.

DAHLIAS are natives of Mexico, Guatemala, Honduras, Nicaragua, El Salvador, and Costa Rica. In addition to conquering the Aztecs, the Spanish brought along botanists who collected plants to bring back to Spain. Around the end of the eighteenth century, dahlias made their way into the hands of Antonio José Cavanilles, the director of the Royal Gardens of Madrid.

He called them "dahlia" after Anders (Andreas) Dahl, a Swedish scientist/environmentalist. Dahlias found their way to Europe around 1790, and by the 1830s, the entire continent fell under their spell. As far as dahlias in America are concerned, no verifiable records exist on specific dates. However, there are varieties recorded here as early as 1821.

Dahlias are long-lasting cut flowers.

Dahlias bring to the table everything you could want in a flower, except for fragrance. Otherwise, they are incredibly diverse. Classified by both the size and the shape of their flower heads, dahlia flower shape classifications include balls, pom-poms, cactus, decorative (informal and formal), singles, semidoubles, collarettes, anemones, stellar, water lily, orchid, and peony types. They come in tall and dwarf varieties, as well as every color you can think of other than blue. If you're still on the fence, then surely their handsome foliage and fast-growing habit will push you over the edge.

Usually grown from tubers or plant cuttings, dahlias can also be started from seed. They are happy in most soil as long as it's well draining. Plant the tubers directly into the garden bed 5 to 6 inches deep. Tubers that haven't sprouted yet tend to rot. So, if the soil tends to stay damp, don't water them until you see shoots. Once the dahlias are actively growing, water them on a regular schedule.

It's true that dahlias need full sun, but they don't like intense heat. Here in my Northern California garden, I plant them where they receive full sun until about 1:30 or 2:00 p.m. to protect them from our brutal afternoon sun. I also add a couple inches of mulch around the base of the plants, which helps keep the soil cool.

Pinch back the first flower stalk that comes up. It'll break your heart, but you'll be rewarded with a bushier plant, which means more flowers. Dahlias are tender perennials, so in cold winter regions (Zones 2 to 7), after the first hard frost (which usually kills off the foliage), tubers should be lifted from the ground, brushed off, and stored in a cool and protected place for the winter.

In mild winter climates (Zones 8 to 11), the tubers can be left to overwinter in the ground. However, it's the smart gardener who will mulch them for the cold months.

It's true that many of the famous dahlia varieties of the 1920s and 1930s are lost to us. However, you can still find the world's oldest surviving dahlia, 'White Aster' (1879), as well as rare varieties like 'Tommy Keith' (1892), 'G. F. Hemerik' (1936), and Jane Cowl (1928) for your garden today.

Tall dahlia varieties grow 2' to 6' tall, while dwarf varieties reach only about 18".

FOXGLOVE
(*DIGITALIS PURPUREA*)

Foxgloves are fabulous in a woodland garden setting.

YOU MAY KNOW *Digitalis purpurea* as common foxglove, glove-of-our-lady, or fairy's thimbles. Each one of these names makes sense in a more or less obvious way. The word *fox*, in this case, could have evolved from the Middle English "folks." The reference would then be of garden fairies donning flowers as gloves. Of course, if we are to entertain the idea of fairies in hand accessories, then it doesn't seem like that much of a leap to envision forest foxes wearing them either.

What you may not know is some of the darker names that she has been given. In 1785, Scottish botanist/scientist/physician William Withering formally introduced digitalis's medical use (digitoxin and digoxin extracts are still used today). Medical advances aside, all parts of foxglove are quite poisonous, which has been common knowledge since the Dark Ages (literally). Thus, our lovely lady was also saddled with such monikers as witches' gloves, bloody fingers, and dead man's thimbles in Ireland. Still, the idea of foxes sporting soft flower gloves tickles me to no end. Best visual ever.

There are digitalis species that are native to Asia and Africa, but *D. purpurea* is native to Britain. It's a biennial plant that produces soft-leaved rosettes the first year and blooms in the second year. Foxglove blooms in early to midsummer with 3- to 6-foot spikes that are densely covered in white, cream, rose, yellow, and light to dark pink flowers, all of which have freckled throats.

Seeds are often started in the spring, but you can give them a leg up by starting them in the fall. When the pods open in late summer, plant them by pressing the seeds into a container of moist

Digitalis purpurea is native to Britain.

soil and don't cover them—light is necessary for their germination. Keep the soil damp and let them overwinter in a cold frame or another protected area.

In the spring, plant the seedlings 18 inches apart from each other in a semishady position in the garden. The soil should be rich with organic matter and be kept damp. Foxgloves enjoy their soil with a side of compost and fertilizer, so be generous. Although biennial, the plants will reseed themselves readily once they are in your garden, and create a foxglove colony that produces flowers every year. If you only plant one foxglove variety, make it the classic, *D. purpurea* 'Alba'—she's stunning.

Cut the flower spikes from the plant once you see a few blossoms open up at the bottom of the stem. This timing does two things. First, it encourages side shoots on the plant, extending the plant's bloom time. Second, it's the best chance that the bees haven't pollinated the flowers yet. Unpollinated flowers have the longest vase life.

D. purpurea reseeds readily to create a foxglove colony.

NOTE

Digitalis is incredibly poisonous. Think twice before planting foxglove in a garden that often hosts children or pets.

Research Unfamiliar (Potentially Invasive) Plants

If you're reading this book, chances are you'll eventually head out in search of flowering plants that are not already growing in your yard or garden. Here's some sound advice: do a little bit of research before you fill your car with unfamiliar plants. Look them up and cross-reference (check a second resource) on reliable databases so that you become familiar with their habits in your region. Most of the time, there won't be an issue. However, you might happen upon a plant that was suggested by someone (ahem) who lives in an area in which that particular plant has zero ill effects. But in your area, that same plant might end up being an invasive, noxious weed that is hell-bent on crowding out your local native plant species. If this happens, you will have your entire town in an uproar. Like a modern-day Frankenstein's monster, they will come for you with pitchforks and torches. You will become a social outcast and your good name will be ruined.

Don't be a monster. Irresponsible planting is a no-win for everybody.

Start here:

- National Invasive Species Information Center

  www.invasivespeciesinfo.gov/resources/databases.shtml

- United States Department of Agriculture (USDA) Database

  www.plants.usda.gov/java/noxiousDriver

Toxic Situations

Let's talk about the word *toxic*. *Toxic* is often used interchangeably with *poisonous*, and *poisonous* tends to infer a life-threatening situation. In the spirit of brutal honesty, let's make things perfectly clear:

- There are plants that have such high levels of toxins (or a specific toxin) that, if ingested, can absolutely kill you.

- There are also plants that have small amounts of toxins (or one that's less dangerous) that might not kill anything, yet could cause skin rashes, stomach or intestinal upset, and so forth, which isn't much fun either.

- Plants can have toxins in one or more of their parts. For example, sometimes it's just the plant's seeds that are toxic, and sometimes the toxins are in the leaves, flowers, and seeds.

- Much of the time, we know which plants these are and which part of the plant should not be touched. However, although a plant is considered nontoxic in general, this is not a guarantee that an individual won't happen to be allergic to (or irritated by) it.

In this book, for any plant that is known to be toxic in general, I will make a note of it in the plant profile. You and your family are not going to put plant parts into your mouth unless it's a known food plant.

But even if you do read that something is edible, you must able to properly identify every plant that you plan on eating and know whether it's safe for human consumption. If you cannot 100 percent positively ID the plant, then do not put it in your mouth, period.

Cutting and Preserving Flowers for the Vase

Once the flowers are blooming, the next big challenge is to get the longest vase life out of the blossoms. After all, getting them to cutting stage should be celebrated as long as possible! Below are some rules of thumb to keep those posies perky.

Timing is everything.

I'm talking about two types of timing here. The first is about the time of day: don't cut flowers in the sunshine. The best time to cut your flowers is in the early morning or in the evening, when flowers are the most hydrated. Your good timing will have them recovering faster and lasting longer in the vase.

The second timing is about the flower species. Some flowers will open their petals even after they have been cut from the stem and others won't open a smidgen more.

General rules of thumb:

- Individual stem flowers, such as sunflowers, zinnia, calendula, and dahlia, should be cut when they are almost fully open.

- Plants that produce multiple flowers on a single stem, such as larkspur, snapdragon, gladiola, and delphinium, should be cut when one flower bud is open and another bud is showing color. This is the same timing rule for flower cluster types, such as Queen Anne's lace, lilac, and yarrow.

- Peony, iris, tulip, and poppy should be harvested in their bud stage before the flowers open.

Always use clean and sharp pruning shears.

Clean vases and tools.

One of the best and simplest things you can do for fresh cut flowers is to make sure all buckets, vases, and hand pruners are extremely clean (sanitized even). Bacteria are the enemy.

Bring cool water to the garden.

Give your cut flowers a leg up and bring a bucket filled with clean, cool water to the garden. Plunge the stem into the water immediately after each cut.

Make good cuts.

The first step to a good cut is clean and sharp pruning shears. Leave the scissors in the house. Cut the flower off as far down the stem as possible. The longer the stem, the more you have to work with when you arrange them. Slice those bad boys off at an angle, remove all foliage that would otherwise end up under water, and place them directly into your water bucket.

Relax and rejuvenate.

Of course, you can always arrange your flowers in a vase right after harvesting. But why not give them a little power nap first? Placing them in a cool, shaded, well-ventilated area for 2 to 3 hours allows them to "condition" (rehydrate) and helps them last longer. Once they are done conditioning, cut 1 inch off the bottom of the stem just before arranging.

Woody stems.

Heirloom flowers such as hydrangea and lilac have woody stems and have a harder time taking up water. Help them out by clipping vertically into the bottom of the stems (making little slits in the wood).

About preservatives.

The best thing I can tell you about commercial floral preservatives (flower food) is that I like them. In addition to a little sugar and acidifier, they contain a biocide. They certainly prolong the life of my cut flowers better than any home concoction I have tried. Get yourself some.

Messy drinkers.

There are some flowers that gunk up vase water in a hurry. They can't help it—it's just who they are. If you're working with sunflowers, zinnias, or rudbeckia, feel free to add a few drops of bleach to the water.

Change the water.

Change the vase water every day and trim about ½ inch off the bottom of the stems each time to make it easier for them to take up more water.

Just say no to fruit and flowers.

Don't keep fruit near your flowers. Ripening fruits such as apples and bananas let off ethylene gas. Ethylene gas is a flower murderer. *Capisce?*

Yesterday's heirloom flowers combine beautifully with today's modern varieties.

GLADIOLA

(*GLADIOLUS* SPP.)

Gladiolas represent sincerity, character, and moral integrity.

IN ANCIENT times, gladiolas were called *xiphium* and acquired their name from the Greek word *xiphos*, which means "sword." Their common name today is, of course, sword lily. Gladiolas are South African natives that were first brought to Europe during the eighteenth century. Those first gladiolas were once the bane of the farmer's existence, as they were an undesirable weed out in the cornfields. (Keep in mind that during that time, the flowers were nearly nondescript.)

Early hybridizers focused on creating plants with more attractive blooms, and eventually gladiolas became desirable. In fact, even before the twentieth century they were already enjoying some good times, and were quite popular in cottage gardens.

Through no fault of their own, gladiolas became the cornerstone flower for funerals. Gladiolas represent sincerity, character, and moral integrity, which might explain why people chose them to represent their loved ones at their final resting place. Still, sadness, mourning, and death make for a dreary connection for a sunny garden flower.

Happily, gardeners' attraction to the elegant, stately stems is coming full circle. And why not? From the middle of summer until frost, gladiolas make for long-lasting cut flowers in the vase. Individual blooms last 6 or 7 days, but an entire stalk can last for weeks. Flower spikes are 36 to 48 inches tall and come in pink, rose, red, orange, salmon, green, yellow, cream, purple, and bicolors—almost any color you can think of other than true blue.

Gladiolas are grown from corms (not bulbs) and should be planted in full sun, 2 to 6 inches deep and 4 to 6 inches apart in fertile, well-draining soil. Sandy loam is ideal. However, it's more important to at least avoid planting them in cold, heavy, wet soils, which can cause the corms to rot. Water them right after planting, but don't begin a regular watering routine until you see shoots pushing up. A nice layer of mulch will help keep the soil moist and keep down competitive weeds. A spot that's protected by a wall (or other barrier) at the back of the bed is optimal because a strong wind will easily mow them down.

Plant glad corms after the last frost date in your area. Stagger as many plantings as you can, getting them into the ground a week apart each time to produce a continuous flower show.

Glads make for long-lasting flowers in the vase.

Cut flower spikes for the vase when the first flowers begin to open. Leave several leaves behind on the plant to serve as an energy source for future blooms. Gladiolas can be left in the ground in the milder Zones 8 to 10. However, in colder areas, they should be lifted from the ground once the leaves have turned brown. Let the corms air-dry for a few weeks in a protected, well-ventilated area, then store them in a mesh bag or a wood box filled with sawdust until the spring.

Most of the heirloom glads you'll find today will be those hybridized after 1930. Old House Gardens, however, has a few oldies worth checking out. One unique-looking glad called 'Abyssinian Gold' is from 1888 and is actually fragrant!

If your tastes favor the bold and bright, *G. byzantinus*, also known as hardy gladiola or Jacob's ladder, might be the perfect glad for your garden. Heralding from Turkey in 1629, this hardy gladiola blooms in vivid magenta in the late spring to early summer.

Wind is gladiola's mortal enemy.

HOLLYHOCK
(ALCEA ROSEA)

Hollyhock with classic single flowers

An entire field of charming hollyhocks

DESPITE her dramatic flower spikes, the sweet and stately hollyhock will never be crowned the queen of the garden. The truth is that the hollyhock is easy to grow and everybody's had her, making her a rather common girl. In no way am I slighting this cottage beauty—she's a required staple in the garden, if you ask me. In the plant world, "common" equals strong, reliable, and fertile. Common is good, so let it go.

Eons ago (like in the sixteenth century), Europeans visited China and returned with—among other fabulous flora—hollyhock seeds. The hollyhock made her way to America via European settlers, and she quickly became the girl-next-door: sweet, unassuming, and trustworthy.

Hollyhock's 5- to 9-foot flower spikes blossom in white, yellow, light pink, pinkish red, burgundy, magenta, and black (okay, deep burgundy). They show up all summer and can be found in the classic single form or in layers of frilly doubles. Although newer varieties have been bred to flower their first year,

heirloom hollyhocks are generally biennial plants. For the most part, during the first year they concentrate on growing leaves and a robust root system. On occasion, they might flower lightly that first year. Your true flowery reward will show up in the second year.

In my mild California climate, hollyhock is free to let her hair down and be who she really is—a short-lived perennial. After their first season in my garden, they flower every year for several years before giving in and passing the torch to the next generation.

Hollyhocks will grow just about anyplace their seeds land. However, a nice spot of sun (or light shade) with deep, fertile, and well-draining soil will have her producing at her best. Seeds can be started in containers indoors, but they do just as well when planted directly into the garden where they will live out their lives. Plant them outside a couple of weeks before the last frost about 24 inches apart. Hollyhock seeds need a little sunlight to germinate, so don't cover them entirely with soil—just sprinkle lightly over the top, kind of like how you're supposed to sprinkle Parmesan cheese on your spaghetti (if you're not me).

Water plants deeply and regularly ("regularly" will be defined by your climate). During the height of summer, I may water them twice a week or more. Soaker hoses and drip systems are your friend. Don't use overhead sprinklers, because watering overhead encourages hollyhock's enemy #1—rust.

Rust is an ugly blight on a pretty face. Unattractiveness aside, rust can take down a plant if left to its own devices. Instead of using chemical controls, I choose to manage it by watering at the roots of the plant, being careful not to splash on the leaves. When I see the smallest sign of rust (orange-brown spots) on the plant, I immediately remove the affected leaves.

Feed plants every 2 to 3 weeks with an organic fertilizer that focuses on flowering plants (lots of phosphorus). Look for fertilizers that have a higher middle number on the bag—for example, 15-30-15. Top-dress garden soil regularly with compost.

Hollyhocks are enthusiastic self-seeders and produce a boatload of discus-shaped seeds. Historically, hollyhocks have been associated with fertility and wealth. This may be true, but reputations are fickle and the hollyhock is better known for perhaps a more basic human need—the bathroom. Or more specifically, the outhouse.

Before the luxury of indoor plumbing, hollyhocks were planted around the outhouse so that when a lady visitor felt nature's call, she wouldn't have to be so crass as to ask someone to point her in the right direction. Tall, colorful spikes would be there like a prim guide, waving her over to the potty place. Others say the flowers were planted around the perimeter to hide the smelly little building. In any case, we now associate hollyhocks with women looking around frantically for somewhere to pee.

The double flower puffs of 'Chater's Double Mix'. Resistance is futile.

HYDRANGEA

(*HYDRANGEA* SPP.)

Bonus: Hydrangeas make gorgeous dried flowers!

NOTHING does what billowy hydrangeas can do for the vintage garden. Like a loving squeeze against a grandmother's bosom, hydrangeas make for bold yet soft blooms, both in the perennial bed and in the vase.

Hydrangeas are native to southern and eastern Asia, as well as America. While we have Asia to thank for bigleaf hydrangea (*H. macrophylla*) and Pee Gee hydrangea (*H. paniculata*), the United States' claim to hydrangea fame is the oakleaf hydrangea (*H. quercifolia*) and Annabelle hydrangea (*H. arborescens*). In fact,

England got its first glance when a colonist brought a native hydrangea home from America in 1736.

The French or bigleaf species is usually what comes to mind when we think of hydrangeas. Also known as florist's hydrangea, this is the one that can be manipulated to bloom blue or pink by altering the pH of the soil—*unless* you have a white-flowered bigleaf, that is. White *H. macrophylla* always bloom white, no matter what. (Try to keep up.) It's hardy in Zones 5 to 9.

Bigleaf hydrangeas can be manipulated to bloom pink or blue depending on the soil's pH.

Some gardeners like to play the alchemist and manipulate their bigleaf's summer flowers to shift from pink to blue and vice versa. This requires adjusting the soil pH by amending it to either raise the acidity (blue flowers) or raise the alkalinity (pink flowers).

If you want to prune hydrangeas (and you don't have to), things can get a little tricky. Not only do some species bloom from old wood (stems that have been there since at least last season) while others bloom from new wood (stems that grew this season), but also the modern varieties can be different from heirloom types. Many of the modern hydrangeas have been bred to bloom on both old and new wood, which takes the guesswork out of pruning but adds to the confusion. In this case, we're interested in heirloom varieties, so we're following the old-school map here.

There are two types of *H. macrophylla*: lacecaps and mopheads (*H. hortensia*). The lacecaps produce flattened flower heads and the mopheads produce big blossom balls. Bigleaf flowers grow on old wood, so prune them right after the plant is done blooming and the flowers are spent. Pee Gee hydrangeas have cone-shaped, creamy white blossoms in late summer to early fall. Pee Gee's flowers grow on new wood, so prune it in the late winter or early spring. She's hardy in Zones 3 to 8.

Annabelle (or smooth) hydrangea produces spherical, white flowers in the summer. It blooms on new wood and should be pruned in late winter or early spring. It's hardy in Zones 3 to 9. Oakleaf hydrangea blooms with white, conical flowers midsummer to fall. It's hardy in Zones 5 to 9. It flowers on old wood, so prune it after the flower show.

With all the potential pruning confusion, it bears mentioning that although pruning should be performed in a specific season, *deadheading* can be done at any time. Clipping off faded blossoms just behind the flower and in front of the first set of leaves is always acceptable and causes zero problems for future blooms. No harm, no foul.

Pruning, however, involves deeper surgery and has the potential to affect next year's flower performance. When you prune hydrangeas, you cut one-fourth to one-third of the oldest canes to the ground. Cuts should be made above a node. Dead and crossed branches are removed, as well.

Hydrangeas enjoy sunny to part shady areas depending on the zone, so be mindful of your microclimate. In my Northern California gardens, my mopheads melt and eventually fry in the full sun. They want moderately fertile, well-drained soil that's loaded with organic matter. Heads up—hydrangeas love their water. These are not the plants for a xeriscape garden.

Tiny bundles of blossom buds beginning to burst. (Say *that* three times fast.)

LARKSPUR

(*CONSOLIDA AMBIGUA*, FORMERLY *DELPHINIUM AJACIS*)

Consolida ambigua, a.k.a. Delphinium ajacis

"**LARKSPUR**" is a common name that is often shared by the bold, tall-spiked delphiniums, *Delphinium ajacis*, and their informal, shorter cousins, *Consolida ambigua*. The fact that the true larkspurs were once classified as *Delphinium ajacis* further blurred their differences and added to the confusion. I'm not usually a fan of botanists changing up plant names on us (I can't help but feel that this is often done out of sheer boredom), but I am relieved that at some point they reclassified larkspur as *Consolida ambigua*. Larkspur is a hardy annual that offers more relaxed flower spires as compared to the regal flower show of the delphinium. Plus, genuine delphiniums are biennials and perennials.

Personally, I find the mild-mannered larkspur utterly charming. Larkspur caught Thomas Jefferson's eye back in the day at his home in Shadwell, Virginia, and he brought them to his gardens at Monticello, where they were planted in the roundabout flower garden in 1810.

Larkspur is a Mediterranean and southern Europe native. During the seventeenth, eighteenth, and nineteenth centuries, it was as common as a tabby house cat. We gardeners have come full circle—larkspur is cool once again.

It won't surprise you to know that it has several more aliases, including rocket larkspur and Lark's heel (or claw or toe). These names all reference the "spur" that sits directly behind each flower, which resembles both bird's feet and shooting stars equally.

Heirloom larkspur blossoms in purple, lavender, crisp white, light/medium/dark blue, salmon pink, and rosy-mauve. Aside from her sweet flowers, she adds texture to the garden bed with her feathery-fern foliage. It's simply a must for an informal cottage garden.

Larkspur is a cool weather lover and should be planted in early spring or the previous fall for earliest blooms. Plant the tiny seeds directly into in a sunny to part shady garden bed and cover them lightly with soil (remember: Parmesan cheese on spaghetti). You'll reap the best flower show if they are planted *en masse* or in drifts. They prefer sandy soil if they can get it and regular watering—without overwatering—all season.

Be patient with them in the beginning, as larkspur seeds are notoriously slow germinators. Slow, as in they don't rear their little heads for 2 to 3 weeks. Once the first true leaves show up, thin the seedlings so that they are spaced 6 to 8 inches apart. This spacing gives them some elbow room, yet also supports the flower spikes as the plants grow. Larkspur self-sows readily, but not annoyingly so.

Annual larkspur is also called rocket larkspur and Lark's heel.

Larkspur flowers come in purple, lavender, crisp white, blue, salmon pink, and rosy-mauve.

Heirloom larkspur varieties include 'Giant Imperial', which produces blue, pink, carmine, and white flowers; light blue blossomed 'Blue Bell'; 'Bunny Bloom', which comes with little bunny heads tucked into the center of each flower; and 'French Alouette', which is packed with double flowers of white, salmon-pink, pure lilac-blue, rose, and iridescent purple.

NOTE

Please keep all parts of the plant, including seeds, away from children and animals who may put it in their mouths. Larkspur in all its forms is poisonous.

Pincushion Flower

(*SCABIOSA ATROPURPUREA* AND *S. CAUCASIA*)

Scabiosa comes in both annual and perennial versions.

IN 1760, Colonials brought these little sweethearts with them from England to America, and we couldn't be happier for the introduction. As an avid needleworker, I can appreciate the moniker the English bestowed upon this delicate flower. It does, indeed, resemble teeny-tiny pins stuck into a pincushion.

Scabiosa comes in both annual and perennial versions, and there isn't a butterfly out there that can resist it. Historically, scabiosa symbolizes grief or unfortunate love. Thankfully, in this case, our collective memory is short. Dismal associations are no longer linked to this sweet and cheerful blossom.

Mediterranean-born *S. atropurpurea* is the annual species that was introduced to Britain in 1629, and cottage gardens would never be the same. Annual pincushion flowers are 18 to 36 inches tall and bloom in white, blue, pink, dark purple, and dark maroon.

They flower in midsummer through October and have more fragrance than their perennial counterparts.

Perennial pincushion, *S. caucasia*, hails from southwest Asia and Russia. The flower stems are shorter than the annual types, but the flower heads are larger. The midsummer through September blooms are usually light blue but also come in pink or white. Perennial scabiosa can be propagated by division in the spring. Both annuals and perennials make long-lasting cut flowers.

Start seeds indoors 4 to 6 weeks before the last frost. Plant seedlings in well-drained, moderately fertile soil in a sunny to part shady location. Additional compost to the bed benefits them greatly. Once they are established, pincushion flowers are not necessarily thirsty plants and they don't enjoy wet feet. Be sure to cut the open flowers (or deadhead spent ones) to keep the blossoms coming.

Pincushion flower in its first year

POPPY

(*PAPAVER* SPP.)

Once you've had poppies in your garden, you'll never want to be without.

PAPAVER offers a variety of flower colors and shapes, so every heirloom gardener is certain to find one that delights. There are single- and double-petaled poppies; those with glossy, shimmering petals; and frilly crinkled types that you would swear were made of crepe paper. Some produce flower heads at a mere 2 inches wide, while on others the blooms are a whopping 1 foot across. I promise you that once poppies have grown in your garden, you'll never want to be without.

Papaver species typically grown are field poppies (*P. rhoeas*), Iceland poppies (*P. nudicaule*), and Oriental poppies (*P. orientale*). A European native, opium poppies (*P. somniferum*) are just as lovely, but

happen to be illegal to grow here in the United States. The poppy species that captured the imagination of the Dutch Impressionists is the same one that produces some extremely potent narcotics (think: morphine, heroin, opium).

One person's pain-relieving pharmaceutical drug is another person's street addiction. While it's a fact that it is breaking the law to grow opium poppies, it's also a fact that *P. somniferum* has been handed down generation after generation, neighbor to neighbor, and gardener to gardener since something like 3400 BCE. It stands to reason that they will be hanging out in our gardens for a while longer. Just keeping it real.

Annual field poppies (also called "corn" or "Shirley" poppies) are also native to Europe and won't land you in the slammer should you spread them with abandon in your yard. Flowers show up in the late spring through early summer in red, white, and pink with black accent marks. If it's field poppies that catch your eye, know that you're in the finest company. Both Vincent van Gogh and Claude Monet felt compelled to paint them, and Thomas Jefferson made certain to plant them at Monticello.

Iceland poppies are my hands-down favorites. They're as though "class" and "contemporary" got together to make a baby. Bright, crepe-y blossoms of red, orange, pink, and white have an irresistible sophistication about them. Iceland poppies are a tender perennial that are usually treated as hardy annuals. They can take some light frost, but perish in deep freezes.

Oriental poppies are native to the Mediterranean as well as Persia. They are a perennial species that produces light pink and red-orange flowers in late spring or early summer. Oriental poppies are a favorite for many a gardener, including Gertrude Jekyll, one of the most influential designers of the twentieth century. *P. orientale* 'Patty's Plum' was one of her favorites.

Poppy seeds germinate best in cool weather, and the seedlings don't enjoy having their roots jiggled about, so your best bet is to plant them directly into the garden. About 4 to 6 weeks before the last frost date, find a spot in full sun (although Oriental poppies grow well in light/dappled shade). Sprinkle the seeds over well-drained and loamy or sandy soil. Don't cover the tiny seeds, as they need the light to germinate. If you live in an area with mild winters, sow seeds in the fall for early spring blooms. Once seedlings are 1 to 2 inches tall, thin the plants so they are 6 to 10 inches apart.

Poppies are social chameleons and are right at home in both formal and cottage gardens.

Flowering Plant Types

- **Annuals:** Plants that live their life cycle out in a single year or season. Many annuals self-sow (drop seeds) each year.

- **Perennials:** Plants that live for several years or longer. There are also short-lived perennials that live only 2 to 3 years.

- **Biennials:** Plants that focus on growing leaves and strong roots the first year and flower only in the second. Some biennials may self-seed each year.

Iceland poppies (*Papaver nudicaule*)

ROSE

(*ROSA* SPP.)

Cabbage roses are one of the old garden roses developed by Dutch breeders somewhere around the seventeenth century.

Noisette belongs to the Antique roses group.

I'M ONE OF THOSE people who has to be smacked over the head repeatedly with the sage proverbs, such as "Never say never." This particular scenario has been played out in my garden more times than I'd like to admit. When I was growing up in the 1970s and 1980s, hybrid tea roses were the goddesses of the garden. So, when I eventually had a garden of my own, it seemed fitting to include them. Everyone loved hybrid teas, and although I honestly wasn't feelin' it, faking it seemed like the polite thing to do. Quite frankly, I was never properly impressed with the modern rose varieties.

Blasphemy, I *know*.

I decided that roses simply weren't for me. I was the odd woman out—a non–rose garden girl. And then I met some old garden roses and realized that I didn't know nearly enough about the rose world to dismiss them. The takeaway here is not that modern rose varieties are undesirable, but that just because some varieties in a species don't resonate with you doesn't mean none of them will. In other words, "Don't throw the baby out with the bathwater." The garden is chock-full of life lessons, my friends.

I'm going to explain old garden roses here in a nutshell. However, the topic requires much more discussion than what can be provided in this simple profile. I urge you wholeheartedly to dig deeper into the subject (resources in the back of this book) and see if they don't send your heart all aflutter.

Old garden roses consist of a group of rose classes that existed before 1867. As far as most rosarians are concerned, any rose that was introduced before this date is considered an old garden rose, antique, or heirloom. As well, 1867 is the year that the first hybrid tea, 'Le France', was introduced by rosarian Jean-Baptiste André Guillot.

There are two subgroups inside the old garden rose group—the old roses and the antique roses. Roses that were in Europe before the late 1700s are referred to as "old roses." Most of them bloom only once in a season. Old rose classes include, but are not limited to (my clever disclaimer), damask, centifolia (cabbage rose), gallica, damask perpetual/Portland, rambler, and alba.

Antique roses were brought to Europe around 1792 and can be traced back to the China rose (*R. chinensis*). The China rose is the first repeat-blooming rose, and its influence means that most of the roses inside this group will bloom again that same season. Antique rose classes include, but are not limited to, China, noisette, bourbon, tea, and hybrid perpetual.

My hands-down favorites are the cabbage roses. Victorian artists couldn't paint enough of them, and I can understand why. I also adore the polyantha 'Cecile Brunner', introduced by Joseph Pernet-Ducher of France as the "sweetheart rose" in 1881. Later, the climbing version was created from a natural sport from the original shrub. If you live in a mild climate, you'll be utterly charmed by rambler 'Lady Banks' rose (*Rosa banksiae* var. *lutea*). With her sweeping miniature, butter-yellow sprays, she's a vertical vision in the heirloom garden.

Damask rose 'La Ville de Bruxelles' was introduced in 1849.

Most roses need at least 6 hours of full sun and well-drained and reasonably fertile soil to be happy. Top-dress them with rich compost several times a year and organically fertilize them in the spring, midsummer, and late summer. As a general starting point, roses should be given 2 to 3 inches of water per week. The watering schedule should be modified based on your soil type and climate. Planting roses so they have some elbow room around their neighbors will promote good air circulation to help keep diseases at bay.

'Louise Odin' is a Bourbon rose from 1851.

Rose Water

Rose water has been used as a beauty treatment for ages. One of the simplest ways is as a natural skin freshener, toner, and hydrator. Then-reigning Egyptian beauty Cleopatra claimed rose water as being one of her primary beauty secrets. If it's good enough for Cleo, it's good enough for me.

To make rose water: Place 1 cup of fresh, organic rose petals in a pan and add enough distilled water to just cover the rose petals. Turn on the heat to low, and place the lid on the pan. You want the water hot, but not simmering. Once the flower petals are almost transparent, strain the liquid into a sterile jar using a fine-mesh strainer. Store the jar of rose water in the refrigerator. It will keep for 4 to 6 weeks. You can also find a pretty spray bottle that's handy for spritzing your face. However, the rose water will only last a couple of weeks outside of the refrigerator.

SNAPDRAGON

(*ANTIRRHINUM MAJUS*)

Pinch the throat of the flower to make the dragon jaws open and snap shut.

CHILDREN know that if you pinch the throat of a single flower, the "jaws" of the dragon open and snap shut. If your children *don't* know this, run out to the garden and show them this immediately. I'll wait.

This southern Europe and Mediterranean native is a staple of the cottage garden. And so should she be. Snapdragons channel the quintessential grandmother, all cheerful, warm, and comforting. An interesting note—the opposite of what's true for most heirloom plants—is that the early snaps were scentless. It wasn't until 1963 that the first fragrant varieties were introduced. That definitely seems like an improvement, but on the other hand the "butterfly" types that were bred to put on a dazzling show lost their characteristic dragon snap in the translation.

In any case, you're going to want these cool weather lovers in your spring garden. Snaps are short-lived, tender perennials that are typically treated as annuals. There are dwarf, medium, and tall varieties that grow from 10 to 36 inches tall. Snaps come in colors of pink, white, orange, apricot, yellow, purple, and bicolors. Seeds can be started either in the fall for early spring blooms or in early spring for later blooms. Plant seeds indoors 8 to 12 weeks before the last frost. Fill a container with damp seed-starting mix and press the seeds into the soil. Don't cover them, as they need light to germinate.

Plant seedlings 6 to 8 inches apart in the garden in full sun or light shade. They prefer richly amended soil if they can get it, but a well-draining one is a must. They bloom in early spring through early summer, and if the spent flowers are cut from the plant (before going to seed), they may rebloom again in the fall. Pinching off the first flowering stem will encourage a bushier plant.

Harvest snapdragons as a cut flower when two-thirds of the flowers are open on the stalk. Look for these standouts: the dark crimson variety called 'Black Prince' and the soft pink-petaled 'Apple Blossom'.

Cut them for the vase when two-thirds of the flowers are open.

Snapdragons are cool weather lovers.

SUNFLOWER
(*HELIANTHUS ANNUUS*)

Sunflowers give novice gardeners a confidence boost!

SUNFLOWERS are native to North America and have been utilized by Native Americans in every way possible—grinding the seeds to make flour, pressing them for oil, and extracting pigments from petals and seed shells to make textile dyes.

Is it true that sunflower faces follow the sun east to west throughout the day? The answer is yes (sort of). Actually, *young* sunflowers follow the sun by stretching the growing stem. Their internal clocks respond to environmental cues that help regulate the plant's growth. Once the sunflower is mature, her flower will face east. It would seem this perpetual east-facing position is not by accident. Flowers facing the east heat up the fastest, and pollinating insects spend more time on warm flowers.

Clever girls.

Sunflowers bloom from July to September and sometimes beyond. Depending on the variety, they may grow from 3 feet tall to an amazing 12 feet tall! Sunflowers are some of the most forgiving plants as far as growing conditions go. They are heat- and drought-tolerant, and they basically need only soil, sun, and a little water. Seeds can be started indoors 4 weeks before the last frost, but I find they do better when they are started directly in the garden bed after the last frost. Plant them 4 inches apart and water them so the soil stays lightly damp until they germinate. Although they appreciate regular watering, sunflowers don't like to be overwatered or overfertilized. (In fact, I have never fertilized my sunflowers at all.)

Sunflowers are such agreeable plants that they give new gardeners a nice confidence boost. If you're a bird lover, sunflowers are a magnet in the garden. Depending on where you reside, look for house finches, titmice, cardinals, chickadees, goldfinches, grosbeaks, nuthatches, pine siskins, and woodpeckers flocking to your sunflower patch.

Sunflowers come in all sizes and a good variety of colors. Some are short, some are tall; they include small heads and huge heads; colors may be yellow, gold, orange, brown, rust, maroon, white, or bicolored. Classic varieties include 'Giant Titan' (12 to 14 feet tall, massive flower heads), 'Autumn Beauty' (5 to 7 feet tall), 'Evening Sun' (6 to 7 feet tall), 'Lemon Queen' (5 to 7 feet tall), and 'Velvet Queen' (5 to 6 feet tall).

Helianthus annuus is a North American native.

ZINNIA

(*ZINNIA ELEGANS*)

'Benary's Giant' is a classic and disease-resistant zinnia variety.

NAMED for eighteenth-century German botanist Johann Gottfried Zinn, *Zinnia elegans* was first introduced to European gardens in 1796 courtesy of Mexico. There were other natives around before this, but their flowers were nothing to write home about. *Z. elegans*, also called youth and old age, was where the good stuff began. Early zinnias were all single-petaled versions, but by 1856 the double-petaled varieties showed up, and our garden cups runneth over. Like sunflowers, zinnias are nearly foolproof and are a real shot in the arm as a gardening confidence booster.

By the way, people aren't the only ones who get a kick out of bright, happy, good-natured zinnias. Butterflies actually worship them as the nectar gods that they are. Flower colors include vivid yellow, orange, white, red, rose, pink, purple, lilac, and multicolored blooms. Varieties include both miniatures and giants that range from about 1 foot to over 3 feet tall.

Seeds can be started indoors 4 to 6 weeks before the last frost. They aren't thrilled about having their roots disturbed, but I often start them this way and they do just fine. If you choose to start them indoors, be sure to wait until their first set of true leaves shows up before you harden them off outdoors. Planting the seeds directly into the garden bed is the easiest.

Well-draining, loamy soil that's loaded with organic matter (compost) will have them at their best. But they are very forgiving plants and do their best to show up no matter where you plant them.

Zinnias make fabulous cut flowers and have a long vase life.

Zinnias bloom from early summer all the way to frost.

Zinnias are annual heat lovers and come into their own when outdoor temperatures soar. The main bugaboo with them is their tendency to contract powdery mildew on their leaves. Planting them 12 inches apart will offer good air circulation and help ward it off. Watering at the base of the plants (root zone), as opposed to overhead watering, will also discourage powdery mildew. Plant them every 2 weeks all summer long and you will never be without blooms. For tall varieties, pinch off the center flower bud when it reaches 12 to 18 inches tall. This will encourage side shoots (more flowers) and a bushier plant.

Zinnias make fabulous cut flowers and have a long vase life if they are harvested at the right time. Renowned flower farming guru Erin Benzakein (Floret Flower Farm) offers this advice on harvesting zinnias: Grab the zinnia stem about 8 inches down from the flower head and give it a gentle shake. If the stem drops or bends, it's not ready to be a cut flower yet. If the stem remains stiff and erect, it's ready to harvest for the vase.

Some classic heirloom zinnias are 'Benary's Giant', 'Cut and Come Again', and 'Persian Carpet'.

MAKING A SUMMER FLOWER CROWN

Flower crowns have been a meaningful part of traditions and ceremonies for centuries. They've been a part of weddings, midsummer celebrations, May Day, and other festivals and special events all over the world.

Flower crowns have something a bit magical about them, and we find them irresistible to this day.

Incorporated into bridal showers, birthdays, and anniversaries, they are simple to assemble. Create a few from your heirloom flower garden for yourself and gift some to friends.

There are many ways to create a beautiful flower crown. I learned to make them while working for a florist as a teenager, and this is still one of the easiest techniques I've found.

MATERIALS

Measuring tape

Thick floral wire (I like 22-gauge)

Wire cutters

1 roll of green floral tape

Floral snips or shears

Ribbons

Hot glue gun (optional)

Focus flowers: You'll need an odd number of "focus flowers," as they will be the focal points on the crown.

Filler flowers: These flowers should be smaller than the focus flowers so that they accent the main ones.

Greenery: This will create the "base" in which the flowers will be placed.

1   Begin by measuring the circumference of your head with the measuring tape. Whether you'd like the crown to sit high or low, make sure the tape is sitting exactly where you'd like the flower crown to sit.

2   Leaving the floral wire attached to the spool, measure out the length needed for your head and then add 1 inch to the length. I like to double my wire base because it gives me more to work with while securing the flowers to the crown. To do this, roll more wire off the spool to the same length you measured before and cut with wire cutters. Bend the entire piece of wire in half. There will be a natural loop at one end. At the *other* end, twist the wire ends together and bend the last 1 inch to form a hook. This is how the crown will hook together.

3   I like to cover the entire base with green floral tape. This ensures that if any part of the base becomes visible at any time, it'll be covered and will blend in. Here's how floral tape works: The adhesive on the tape doesn't work until it is slightly stretched. Use a finger and your thumb to hold onto the tape end at one end (usually against flower stems) and pull the other end taut as you go along wrapping stems (or what have you).

Starting at the loop end of the crown, cover the entire base with the floral tape. It wraps up quickly if you wrap it at an angle as you go.

4   There are two ways to get the flowers onto the crown. I'll describe both ways so you can decide what works for you.

Add the flowers individually:

Starting at one end (using floral tape), add the focal flowers, filler flowers, and greenery individually all the way down the wire, trimming the ends as needed with floral snips. Be sure to place the focus flowers evenly throughout at regular intervals. All the flowers should be facing the same direction as you add them. This method often creates a thinner flower crown (although not necessarily) and is a slower process. However, the flowers will often remain tighter against the crown because the flowers are taped separately.

Add the flowers as tiny bouquets:

Instead of placing the flowers singly onto the wire, you can make a bunch of tiny bouquets. (The completed flower crown in the first photo took eight tiny bouquets.) Simply choose some flowers and use floral tape to wrap the stems to create sweet little bundles. Adding miniature bouquets to the crown speeds up this project. Occasionally, once the crown is placed on a head, a gap in the bouquets may become apparent. If so, adhere one of the flower stems from the next bouquet to the wire, or wrap on an individual flower.

5   Hook the bent end of the wire into the loop at the other end. Finish your flower crown by tying long ribbons from the back; hot gluing two short ribbons and tying them into a bow; or hot gluing flower heads onto the back to hide the hook if necessary.

2

FLOWERS
FOR FRAGRANCE

---

*"Perfumes are the
feelings of flowers."*

—Heinrich Heine

It's impossible to discuss vintage flowers and not talk about scent. First, our sense of smell is oh so closely connected with memory, probably more so than any of our other senses. As we talked about at the beginning of this book, the memory of a garden, plant, or flower is often the first catalyst for our heirloom flower fascination.

Throughout history, fragrant flowers were used to mask the scent of unwashed bodies. Tussie mussies/nosegays were carried and tiny tussies/boutonnieres were worn for this specific function. We had some interesting views on bathing (way) back in the day. For example, at one point, bathing regularly was considered an unhealthy practice. During the sixteenth century, many areas in Europe believed that bathing opened the pores, allowing not only diseases that came from the water to enter the body, but also allowing any disease or infection traveling through the air to enjoy easy entry to the body. Depending on the country and the era, people might have bathed once or twice a month—or sometimes twice a year. The body odor must have been insane.

The fragrant flowers in the garden were the nose's only defense. During the English-Georgian period (1714–1760), carrying a tussie mussie or nosegay made from a handful of scented posies became a popular technique to disguise body odors—at least a little bit. Tussie mussies were, perhaps, best at protecting the holder's nose from the ripe scent of others, as opposed to masking their own body odors. Thankfully, we have evolved into an age of some pretty decent hygiene. Aside from unbathed bodies, tussie mussies covered up other unpleasant smells, such as the odors of illness and death.

Today we enjoy fragrant heirloom flowers to relax us, lift our spirits, and put us in a better mood. Evening strolls in the garden are more romantic when night-scented flowers such as sweet rocket and flowering tobacco perfume the air. Which flowers smell the best? Scent, like beauty, is in the nose of the beholder. Still, some flowers, such as roses and lilacs, practically have a cult following. At the top of my personal list are stocks (annual), pink jasmine, and honeysuckle.

To breathe in beauty all season long, plant fragrant flowers that bloom at different times from spring to fall. You can strategically place pots and containers near windows and doorways to take full advantage of the plants. In early spring, we always have potted stock by the front door, which brings a burst of perfume whether we are coming or going. Jasmine has been intentionally planted outside our master bedroom window for the same reason.

Bee Balm
(*MONARDA DIDYMA*)

Monarda didyma is an enthusiastic spreader.

Hummingbirds, bees, and butterflies all pay homage to bee balm.

MONARDA DIDYMA is known by many common names, including bee balm, bergamot, scarlet bee balm, horsemint, and Oswego tea. This distinctive perennial is a North American native that's well known for its many medicinal properties, including (but not limited to) as an antifungal, an antimicrobial, a relaxing nervine, and a digestive aid.

Bee balm belongs to the mint family and is said to be instrumental in soothing stomach upset, bronchial issues, menstrual cramps, and headaches. Monarda also produces high concentrations of thymol (as in thyme), which is a strong antiseptic.

Bee balm is clearly not a one-trick pony. As far as fragrance goes, you'll find that the fruity orange scent is strongest in the leaves, not the flowers. The fraggle-topped blossoms are a happy bonus (you're welcome). From late June through August, bee balm produces 3- to 4-foot-tall flower stems. On top of those stems sit floppy clusters of true red, Dr. Seuss–like hairdos. I mean upright, tubular flowers. Of course, we now have monarda varieties that also bloom in purple, white, salmon, and pink. But the old-fashioned, brilliant red

is outstanding. Bonus: If you enjoy wild critters in your garden as much as I do, you'll be happy to know that bees, butterflies, and hummingbirds pay homage to the aromatic herb.

The easiest way to propagate monarda is by division or taking cuttings. They can also be directly seeded into the garden bed after the last frost date. Choose an area that has full sun or partial shade. Plant seeds, cover them lightly, and keep them moist until they germinate. Once they are several inches tall, thin plants to 18 to 21 inches apart from each other. Bee balm prefers rich, well-draining, moist soil to be at its best. Plant it near a walkway where human hands can't help but brush the leaves (and release the aroma) as they pass by.

I think it's only fair to caution you that *M. didyma* can be a *little* overly enthusiastic about its survival. Plainly speaking, depending on the environment, bee balm can be an aggressive grower. The plant can spread rapidly through underground stems (stolons). It's not necessarily anything to panic about—just keep your eye on it.

Flowering Tobacco

(NICOTIANA ALATA)

Nicotiana alata's trumpeted flowers open and release their scent in the evening.

Flowering tobacco is also called jasmine tobacco, winged tobacco, and night-scented tobacco.

FLOWERING tobacco—also called jasmine tobacco, winged tobacco, and night-scented tobacco—is native to southern Brazil, Argentina, Uruguay, and Paraguay. In the sixteenth century, Jean Nicot introduced flowering tobacco to Catherine de' Medici and the French court, and it was used as a snuff for the queen's migraine headaches. Although it is in the same family, the ornamental species *N. alata* doesn't produce the amount of nicotine that's found in *N. tabacum*, which is the species harvested for tobacco products.

Grown as an ornamental since the 1800s *N. alata* is a tender perennial that's usually treated as an annual. Its star-shaped, trumpeted flowers open in the evening and release a jasmine scent into the night air. Tightly closed until the afternoon, flowering tobacco blooms can look a bit drowsy in the light of day. *N. alata*'s flowers are typically white; however, you can also find blooms in pink, purple, red, and creamy greenish.

Nicotiana's green parts leave a little to be desired and can at best be described as gangly. There's nothing cuddly about this plant. The leaves and stems are actually sticky, but don't get me wrong—its perfume is downright intoxicating and well worth a little homeliness. I do tend to tuck a little something in front of them for additional substance. Flowering tobacco's sweet perfume attracts many night-pollinating insects from July to October. However, it's primarily pollinated by hummingbirds and their lookalikes, the sphinx or hawk moths.

Nicotiana prefers a fairly fertile soil (add compost), regular watering, and a sunny to partly sunny position in the garden. Hint: A spot where there's some protection from strong afternoon sun will coax the flowers into opening up a little earlier. Start seeds indoors 8 weeks before the last frost in your area. Press seeds into moist seed mix, but don't cover the seeds, as they need sunlight to germinate. Seeds can also be sown directly into the garden bed after the frost date has passed. Plant them 12 to 18 inches apart in the garden. Nicotiana self-seeds readily.

HELIOTROPE
(*HELIOTROPIUM ARBORESCENS*)

Heliotrope is also called cherry pie plant for good reason.

Want to know what heliotrope flowers smell like? Its common name is a dead giveaway: cherry pie plant. Yes, folks: warm cherry pie, baked apples, warm vanilla, and vanilla merengue are all delicious ways people describe the heavenly scented heliotrope. Those who are less food-oriented are inclined to liken the scent to almonds or violets (both of which are still edibles, by the way). The description might also change with the clock, because heliotrope's scent is prone to change slightly throughout the day depending on the temperature. In any case, you need this fragrant heirloom flower in your life.

In the 1700s this Peruvian native was collected by French botanist Joseph de Jussieu and by 1757 was well established in British gardens. Thomas Jefferson had seeds from herbe d'amour (flower of love) sent from France to Monticello in 1786.

Cherry pie plants are perennials usually grown as annuals, and they reach 10 to 30 inches tall. Scent aside, heliotrope flowers show up as velvet-clustered flower heads up to 15 inches across. They bloom from June to hard frost, mostly in deep purple but also lavender, lilac, blue, and white. *Heliotrope arborescens* are handsome plants (even without the flowers) and thrive in containers.

Start seeds indoors at least 10 weeks before the last frost date. Press seeds into damp seed-starting mix, but don't cover the seeds, as they need light to germinate. Cover the seed tray with clear plastic to keep the medium damp. You're going to need a little patience to be rewarded by this one—it can take 2 to 4 weeks for heliotrope to germinate. Plant seedlings in a sunny spot with organically rich and well-draining soil. In extremely hot areas, plant them in semishade. Pinch the plants to promote bushiness.

Heliotrope's fragrance is nothing short of euphoric.

LILAC

(SYRINGA VULGARIS)

Lilac blossoms are so worth the wait.

Lilacs need 7 hours of full sun to produce flowers well.

SYRINGA VULGARIS is the species known as the common lilac. She's a long-lived, deciduous shrub that's native to the Balkans in southeastern Europe. *S. vulgaris* was brought to Vienna by respected plantsman Ogier Ghiselin de Busbecq in 1592. Soon after, the new girl landed in Britain and quickly rose in popularity, and by the early 1600s, she had managed to naturalize herself in her adopted home. Soon after, lilac naturalized in her next adopted home, North America.

Lilacs are a multistemmed shrub that can grow to 25 feet tall—but you're not going to let that happen (we'll get to that in a minute). They're easy to grow, drought-tolerant (once established), and long-lived. A lilac is the ultimate proverbial lady, and she'll keep you waiting to enjoy her beauty. You must have patience—*S. vulgaris* is slow to mature and often takes several years for her first flowers to show up, and then there's that short blooming window.

All of this said, *I cannot express enough* how worth the wait she is once her classic feminine blossoms make their appearance. You will forgive her over and over and over again. *S. vulgaris* blooms late spring to early summer, depending on the variety, and 6- to 8-inch-long conical flowers blossom in white, pink, blue, purple, or lilac. The spring lilac fragrance is robust, sweet, and spicy.

From the mid-1800s to the early 1900s, a nursery owned by the Lemoine family in Nancy, France, hybridized the early heirloom lilacs and gave to us at least 153 lilac cultivars, including some with double blooms. You'll find quite a few of them still available to this day, including 'Congo' (1896), a double pink variety; 'Victor Lemoine' (1906), a double blue variety; and 'Belle de Nancy' (1891), a double lilac. 'Lucie Baltet'

(1888), a variety introduced by the Baltet nursery in Troyes, France, produces unusual copper-colored buds that give way to light pink blossoms.

Lilacs need 7 hours of full sun to flower well. If they get less than 7 hours, they will simply end up as lovely, green, shrubby things with, perhaps, a couple of gasping flowers at the very top straining for the sunlight. *No bueno*. The soil should be rich in organic matter, well draining, and a little sweet—while they do their best to please, lilacs prefer a soil that's neutral to slightly alkaline.

Let's talk about pruning. First, there are no laws (anywhere) that say you must prune your lilacs. After all, they have been living and blooming just fine without interfering humans, thank you very much. On the other hand, you probably would like to see flowers in front of your face, where you can enjoy them, rather than 25 feet over your head. This is certainly where your heirloom shrub is heading if it's left forever unattended.

If you've recently planted new lilacs, they won't require pruning or shaping until they are about 6 feet tall. So, new lilac growers get a pass for now. Pruning your lilacs carefully will keep them from becoming the behemoths they are destined to be, and it will rejuvenate the plant for the most flowers possible. Once you've pruned, there should be a mix of stems that are 1 to 2 inches in diameter. Keeping various combined new and old stems will have your lilac plants blooming at their best every year.

Prune mature lilacs *right after* the blossoms have faded. This is important because lilac flowers are produced on old (last year's) wood. If you lollygag around for a few weeks/months and prune too late, you could unwittingly lop off next year's blooms.

What to Do When Pruning Lilacs

- Prune (cut off) off dead and/or diseased stems.

- Prune suckers (sprouts growing off the roots) and twiggy bits.

- Prune stems that are thicker than 2 inches in diameter.

- When removing any stems, cut them off down at the base of the plant (not just the top of the stem).

- Do not prune away more than one-third of the lilac shrub. By the way, you may not have to cut one-third of the plant at all, but don't remove any more than that.

PEONY

(*PAEONIA* SPP.)

Peony blossoms may need support with peony rings.

ANY FLOWER that resembles a generous scoop of fluffy ice cream automatically gets my vote. Judge me if you will, but I'm willing to bet that you also have a little difficulty shoving aside that sweet visual. Peony is a Las Vegas showgirl from the word *go*—but in all the best ways: loud, bold, and flirty, sometimes bordering on brassy. I've heard some varieties described as "gaudy" (just not in front of me).

Originally hailing from Asia, Greece, and outhern Europe, peonies have been protected, cultivated, and otherwise cherished worldwide for over 2,000 years. There are several groups of peonies, including herbaceous, woodland, intersectional, and tree types.

For the purpose of this book, let's talk about the most popular garden type, herbaceous or Chinese peonies.

Herbaceous peonies come in a variety of colors and five flower forms, including single, double, semidouble, anemone, and Japanese. There are various species inside these general types, which is admittedly a bit confusing. In any case, all peonies are grown in the same way regardless of species. Herbaceous peonies are perennial and disease-resistant, and make fabulous cut flowers. They begin blooming from mid-May to early June to summer in Zones 3 to 8, depending on the variety and your zone.

In addition to some of the most beautiful and fragrant blooms anywhere, the peony has shiny, deep green leaves that hang around long after the flowers have become a memory. Hard frosts will cause the leaves to die back to soil level; the growth will reemerge early the following spring (in hardy zones).

Herbaceous peonies can be planted in both spring and fall. The biggest mistake you can make with peonies is planting them too deep. If the tuber is planted deeper than 2 inches under the soil, it won't bloom. If you purchase a peony in a container, set the rootball into the hole and fill it so that the original soil line is flush with your garden soil line. Every peony's dream home is in nutrient-rich, well-draining (no wet feet) soil, situated where it will get at least 5 hours of full sun. However, knowing your area's climate and your garden's microclimate will pay off in spades. While peonies love their sunshine, "full sun" can be an entirely different scenario depending on the growing zone and individual microclimates.

In the far northern states, "full sun" will mean exactly that, so plant them where they receive sun all day long. But if you try that here in Northern California, you'll have fried peony plants. Here, I must plant them where they receive morning sun and dappled sun/shade for the rest of the day. Water them deeply and infrequently.

Peonies are strong, vigorous plants once they are well rooted in your garden. They become fully established and perform at their best after 3 years, but what seems like a significant time investment is certainly worth the long wait. Most herbaceous peonies will need to be staked to support the heavy blossoms. How much support they need is determined by the flower form and the height of the variety. Support the blossoms by using peony rings, tomato cages, or simply bamboo stakes and twine.

Peonies are a beloved foundation in the perennial garden, as they require little maintenance and are extremely long-lived (potentially 100 years—I kid you not). The term *deer-proof* has been tossed around, but I'm skeptical. *Deer-resistant* is probably more accurate. Deer species in Northern California are world renowned for their inability to recognize the plants they shouldn't eat—just fence everything in if deer are a problem.

Treasured herbaceous *Paeonia lactiflora* varieties include the early blooming 'Festiva Maxima', late bloomer 'Sarah Bernhardt', long-lasting 'Gay Paree', bold red 'Lord Kitchener', double-petaled 'Irwin Altman', and one of Monet's favorites (both to grow and to paint), the snow white 'Duchesse de Nemours'.

Peony plants are extremely long-lived.

Bring your peonies in and show them off!

Phlox
(*PHLOX PANICULATA*)

Phlox is long-blooming and long-lived. You need this perennial in your garden.

IT'S INTERESTING that nobody has come up with a clever or fun common name for tall garden/summer/border phlox. These plain-vanilla names feel like proof that everyone is somehow overlooking this sweetheart of a workhorse. The truth is that we weren't impressed with them from the start. *Phlox paniculata* is a North American native that was exported to Europe and first recorded in Britain in 1732. During the late 1800s, phlox was exported (re-exported?) back to America. Everyone was pleased as punch to have them in their gardens once they were reintroduced from Europe. Typical.

Phlox brings it all to the garden. She's a hardy, long-blooming, long-lived perennial. In late spring or early summer, she produces some seriously fragrant flower clusters on 3- to 4-foot-tall flower stalks of white, pink, periwinkle, purple, lavender, and magenta. Rich soil that's kept moist will have her producing heavily for weeks on end. What's not to love?

Powdery mildew, that's what's not to love. Phlox can be prone to it, and although the fungal disease probably won't kill the plant, it is unsightly and can mess up the flower heads to boot. Preventive measures include watering at the root zone (as opposed to overhead), spacing plants to allow for good air circulation, watering early in the day so any wet leaves can dry quickly, taking care not to overfertilize, and removing any plant debris affected by the fungus.

The best way to propagate plants is by division (every 3 to 4 years) in spring or fall. Cuttings can also be taken and rooted in the summertime. Plant phlox 18 to 24 inches apart to provide good air circulation and combat mildew. Deadhead phlox to encourage more blossoms.

Phlox paniculata can grow to 4' tall.

Edible Heirloom Flowers

Some flowers are just begging to be brought into the kitchen and served up with your favorite culinary dishes. Edible heirloom flowers can be used in salads, salad dressings, bean dishes, rice dishes, frozen ice cubes, soups, pasta, omelets, sauces, pizza, syrups, cookies, cakes, artisan sugars, vegetables, butters and other spreads, and as a fresh garnish in summer drinks.

- Bee balm (*Monarda didyma*)
- Calendula (*Calendula officinalis*)
- Cornflower (*Centaurea cynaus*)
- Daylily (*Hemerocallis* spp.)
- Dianthus (*Dianthus* spp.)
- Gladiola (*Gladiolus* spp.)
- Hollyhock (*Alcea rosea*)
- Honeysuckle (*Lonicera japonica*)
- Johnny-jump-up (*Viola* spp.)
- Lavender (*Lavendula* spp.)
- Lilac (*Syringa vulgaris*)
- Marigold (*Tagetes erecta, T. patula*)
- Nasturtium (*Tropaeolum majus*)
- Peony (*Paeonia lactiflora*)
- Primrose (*Primula vulgaris*)
- Rose-of-Sharon (*Hibiscus syriacus*)
- Roses (*Rosa* spp.)
- Sunflower (*Helianthus annuus*)
- Zinnia (*Zinnia elegans*)

Let's Go Over the "No Excuse Rules for Edible Flowers"

1. Only eat flowers that come from plants that you can 100 percent identify as an edible plant or flower.

2. Eat only the parts of that plant that are known to be safe for human consumption.

3. Never eat flowers that have been sprayed with pesticides or herbicides.

PINKS

(*DIANTHUS* SPP.)

Sweet William (*Dianthus barbatus*)

WHEN it comes to the origin of dianthus, we're apparently long on speculation and short on hard facts. Suffice it to say that most trails lead back to southern Europe. We do know that dianthus can be traced back 2,000 years and that hybrid varieties were already on the scene by 1634. Thomas Jefferson planted both China pinks (*D. chinensis*) as well as sweet William (*D. barbatus*) at his home in Shadwell in 1767 and again at Monticello in 1807. So, yeah, there's no doubt that these guys are as old as dirt.

Pinks have a thick, clove-and-other-spices scent and have a long vase life, making them excellent cutting flowers. There are annual, biennial, and perennial dianthus species that have single, semidouble, and double-petaled varieties. Their blue-gray to gray-green leaves are thin and narrow, and almost grasslike. Dianthus prefers sun (to part shade in the hottest areas) and a well-draining, sandy, and limey soil. The exceptions are *D. barbatus* and *D. plumarius*, which prefer their soil a little richer. Dianthus is happiest in rock garden situations and makes great container plants as well. It's best not to mulch them, as pinks are prone to crown rot.

The name *pinks* refers to the frilly petal edges that look as if they have been cut with pinking shears.

Dianthus goes by many names, including pinks, sweet William, gillyflower, July flower, carnations, China pinks, cheddar pinks, and clove pinks. All are used interchangeably, but technically they each refer to specific dianthus species.

The common name *pinks*, in this case, refers to the frilly edges of the flower petals rather than the color—the petals look as if they have been trimmed with pinking shears. If you don't know what pinking shears are, go ahead and give your mom a call right now. I promise you that she knows. Plus, she needs to dig out that picture of you and your sister in homemade Easter dresses anyway. I'll wait.

D. barbatus (sweet William) is a biennial that's treated as a hardy annual. She's an old cottage-garden staple that produces 18- to 24-inch-tall flowers in early spring to early summer. *D. caryophyllus* (carnations or clove pinks) is perhaps the most well-known dianthus commercially. Lovely, frilly pom-pom heads sit atop a long, sturdy stem. *D. chinensis* (China pinks) are an annual species native to China, Korea, Mongolia, and Russia. Perennial *D. gratianopolitanus* (cheddar pinks) hails from Cheddar Gorge in England, and *D. plumarius*, *D. superbus*, and *D. deltoids* are all perennial species. All are a treat for the nose and all bring in the butterflies.

Dianthus makes a stunning display when planted *en masse*. Start seeds indoors 6 to 8 weeks before the last frost date (cover seeds lightly). Plant seedlings outdoors in early spring about 12 inches apart. Seeds can also be planted directly into the garden bed in the early spring. If you live in a mild winter area, they can be sown in the garden in the fall for blooms the following spring. A simple way to propagate dianthus is by taking stem cuttings from new, spring growth that hasn't flowered yet.

Dianthus has a vase life of 10 to 14 days.

Basic Flower Arranging Principles

Professional floral arranging lessons move well beyond the scope of this book. However, essential design principals are at the heart of every beautiful bouquet. Consider these core elements:

Focal point.

The focal point, or emphasis, is the main feature in the design. The idea is to let the supporting flowers and greenery draw your eye to it. Focal points can be highlighted in various ways, including where the flower (focal point) is placed, as well as color, texture, size, or form contrasts.

Physical and visual balance.

Physical balance means exactly that—the actual distribution of the floral materials in the container (weight). To keep a physical balance, you may need to add a counterweight (other flowers or greens) to the opposite side. Visual balance refers to how well the arrangement is balanced to the eye, creating a pleasing design balance, such as symmetry (balanced equally on both sides—traditional/formal) or asymmetry (materials on either side are unequal—modern/informal).

Proportion and scale.

Proportion and scale are about relationships, and the concepts vary only slightly from one another. Proportion is about the size relationship between the materials you designed with (flowers, container, greenery, and so on). Scale, on the other hand, is about how the completed arrangement relates in size to its surroundings (such as the table).

Harmony.

Harmony is about the colors and textures and how well they are working together to create eye candy in the arrangement. This also extends to the container choice and how well the piece represents its surroundings.

Rhythm.

Rhythm within an arrangement is created by careful placement of plant materials, textures, forms, lines, and so on. The idea is to create a flow for the eye to move around the entire arrangement, usually starting at the focal point, moving around the rest of the piece, and then coming back to rest on the focal point.

12 Quickie Flower Arranging Tips

In lieu of an intricate and extensive professional flower arranging school (which I am not qualified to teach), I offer some fast and furious tips that should culminate in some pretty dandy results.

1.
Try to start with the flowers rather than with the vase or container. Which flowers simply must come into the house? The arrangement can feel stiff and forced if you create around a container.

2.
Now pick your container—it doesn't have to be a vase. Tins, milk bottles, teapots, liquor bottles, mason jars, pitchers, watering cans . . . (you get the idea).

3.
Gather flowers that have interesting or contrasting colors, forms, and textures.

4.
Collect a lot of foliage. It may seem counterintuitive, but greenery gives the arrangement a little somethin'-somethin'. Don't worry about it being the typical bouquet greenery—grab anything interesting that you see (the more texture, the better).

5.
Don't stop at greenery. Berries, seedpods, grasses, woody stems, evergreens, and houseplant foliage are all interesting and will make the arrangement unique. Greenery and other goodies help give the arrangement shape, as well.

6.
God created flower frogs for a reason. Collect and use them.

7.
Large/tall containers are for tall flowers and small/short containers for short flowers. You want the flower height to be in proportion to the container size. In general, the flower should not be more than half as tall as the container.

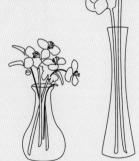

8.
Get rid of all the leaves on the stem that will sit below the water line.

9.
Start the arrangement by placing the tallest flowers (or greenery) first. Arrange the materials that come next in line and so on.

10.
Two practical thoughts: First, remove stamens from flowers that have pollen on them. Pollen is not only messy but can also stain with the best of them. Next, consider where the arrangement will be displayed. Strong-scented flowers are "the bomb," but perhaps not at the dinner table. It's hard to appreciate that badass beef Wellington you've mastered with freesias in your face. Just sayin'.

11.
If you angle the stems as you place them into the vase, you can create a natural "grid" that will support the entire arrangement.

12.
Once you have everything in place, stand back and check out your arrangement from every angle. You're looking for uniformity and repeating patterns.

STOCK

(*MATTHIOLA INCANA*)

Stocks are cool-weather lovers and are exceptional in the spring garden.

MATTHIOLA INCANA is native to southern Europe and named for the Italian naturalist Pietro Andrea Matthioli, who identified it. Once in England, stock was common in gardens by the sixteenth century. Much of every plant's personality can be found in the specific epithet—that is, the second part of its Latin name. *Incana* translates to "gray-white," which refers to stock's leaves.

Stocks are also known as night violets and 10-week stock. Actually, 10-week stock once was defined as a different species (*M. annua*). At some point, it was incorporated into the *M. incana* species (*M. incana* 'annua'), with its variety name offering the only clue to its origination. In any case, stocks' potent, spicy clovelike fragrance is nothing short of euphoric. What I am saying here is to take advantage of the natural high and plant it in pots flanking the front door.

Stock is a cool weather lover that blooms in the lower temperatures of spring and fall. Single or double blossoms produced on spikes can be white, cream, red, purple, pink, or blue. She's fast-growing and can go from seed to bloom in as little as 10 to 12 weeks, which makes her hard to beat as an early season cutting flower. Flowers aside, stock's narrow, grayish green leaves are attractive, as well.

Sow seeds indoors 6 to 8 weeks before the last frost date. They can also be sown directly into the garden bed once the last frost date has passed. That said, you may have more success starting them indoors and transplanting them.

Plant seeds ¼ inch deep in seed-starting mix. Don't let the soil dry out, but don't waterlog the plants either. Even moisture is important to stock seed germination. I should add that some people swear that matthiolas germinate better if they are simply pressed into the soil, allowing light to reach them. Plant the hardened-off seedlings 10 to 12 inches apart in loamy, relatively rich soil (add compost) in full sun or semishade. Considering she really starts to come undone in temperatures over 65°F, semishade is your best bet if you live in an area with short springs and extremely hot summers.

Matthiola incana makes a fabulous cutting flower.

Sweet Pea

(*LATHYRUS ODORATUS*)

Sweet peas are undemanding and easy to grow.

SWEET PEAS came to us through Italy's Father Franciscus Cupani in 1699. He collected the sweet pea seeds and shared them with an English schoolmaster, Dr. Robert Uvedale, and a Dutch botanist, Dr. Caspar Commelin. Next thing you know (bada-bing bada-boom), sweet peas were commercially available by 1724.

Sweet peas are fast-growing, cool-weather annuals. Intensely fragrant and colorful blossoms of white, cream, blue, violet, pink, red, and bicolors are produced on vines that grow up to 6 feet tall. The leaves are bluish green and situated in paired leaflets. Sweet pea's twisty tendrils have a difficult time climbing anything that is slick, but they will make quick work of a support trellis composed of poultry wire. I placed them here in the fragrance chapter, but they are so easy to grow that they could have been added to the Cottage Classics chapter as well.

Sweet peas like at least half a day of sun and full sun, if possible. The reason they can tolerate part shade is that that their ultimate happy place is with their faces warm and their feet cool. Like many flowers, they prefer their soil rich, loamy, and certainly well draining. So, don't be chintzy with the compost.

Although the seeds can be started indoors, it's actually easier to plant them directly into the garden bed. In mild winter areas where the ground doesn't freeze, plant seeds in October–November for early spring flowers. In cold winter areas, plant them as soon as the soil can be worked in the spring. If you soak sweet pea seeds in a bowl of water 24 hours before planting, you'll improve the germination percentage. Regularly harvest sweet pea flowers for the vase (or at least deadhead them) to keep the flowers coming as long as possible.

Some excellent heirloom sweet pea varieties include the following:

- **'Black Knight'** (1898) was introduced by Henry Eckford in 1898. It's extremely fragrant and has dark purple-maroon blossoms.

- **'Cupani'** is said to be the original strain of 1699. Flowers are violet, blue-purple, or bicolored.

- **'Painted Lady'** (1730), also known as 'Old Spice', would have been completely lost to us if an Australian family hadn't saved it from oblivion.

Sweet peas are passionate climbers and will immediately need a support such as a trellis or netting.

May Day Baskets

May Day celebrations have been part of history nearly as long as people have. All are variations of the theme of welcoming the changing seasons—namely, spring. Among the many May Day traditions, such as maypoles, festivals, May queens, goddesses, and social reform, is the simple gifting of the May Day basket. It's a simple tradition well worth bringing back in this modern day.

Fill a wicker basket, tin bucket, or paper cone with flowers and perhaps other goodies such as candies or seed packets. On May 1, leave the May Day basket at a neighbor, friend, or relative's front door. Next comes the best part: ring the doorbell, run, and hide, so you can watch as you brighten someone's day.

Although tussie mussies were predominantly used to disguise odors as you went about your day, the Victorians made them popular as personalized gifts. At that time, each of the flowers used to create the little hand bouquet had a meaning (sometimes several) attached to it. It was a discreet and lovely way to send a message to lovers, friends, and family. For example, a tussie mussie made with red carnation (love, fascination, passion), larkspur (love, strong attachment, affection), and red tulip (romantic intention, passion, affection) would certainly be a declaration of love.

With the comeback of heirloom flowers into home gardens, I am hoping that we can bring back tussie mussies as gifts to those we care about. We have plenty of opportunities to use them! How fabulous would it be to walk into a restaurant for your anniversary dinner holding an anniversary tussie from your husband? (Husbands: Making sure that some of the flowers are the same kind that were in her wedding bouquet will earn you extra points.) How about for someone turning sweet sixteen? Or the bride-to-be at her wedding shower? Or the expectant mom at her baby shower? Birthdays, Mother's Day, and May Day are all excellent reasons to give tussie mussies.

MATERIALS

Focus flowers: You'll need an odd number of "main" flowers that will serve as the focal point of the tussie. Main flowers are the standouts, such as rose, carnation, hydrangea, or purple coneflower.

Filler flowers: These flowers will be smaller and more subdued than the main flowers, and might include species such as statice, lavender, sedum, or foamflower. They are an accent to the main flowers.

Greenery: Greens create the "base" for the other flowers. Consider small shrub branches, evergreens, berries, and herbs.

Green floral tape

Paper doily (optional)

Scissors (optional)

Ribbon

Hat or corsage pin

1   Choose some main flowers for the center of the tussie mussie and strip the leaves from the flower stems.

2   Gather the main flowers together until the shape pleases you (usually this will be a rounded shape). Use the floral tape to secure them together. Here's how floral tape works: The adhesive on the tape doesn't work until it is slightly stretched. Use a finger and your thumb to hold onto the tape end at one end (usually against flower stems) and pull the other end taut as you go along wrapping stems (or what have you).

3   Choose a filler flower or two and strip the leaves off the stem that will be wrapped.

4   Use the floral tape to wrap the filler flowers onto the already wrapped main flowers. Place them randomly around the main flowers for a natural look.

5   At this point, you could add a couple of different main flowers if you'd like. Or move on to the greenery.

6   Choose your greenery and strip the leaves off where they will be wrapped onto the tussie. Place them so that they surround the entire bouquet.

7   Wrap the entire tussie mussie with the green floral tape.

8   If you want to use the doily as a collar for your tussie, cut an X into the middle of the doily and slide it onto the stems. Push it up until it's hugging the flowers.

9   To give the bouquet a finished look, start at the bottom of the stems and wrap the ribbon around itself a couple of times to secure the end.

10   Keep wrapping the stems all the way to the top with the ribbon, angling it so that it slightly overlaps to cover the floral tape. Once at the top, give it a couple more wraps, coming back down the stems. Secure with a hat or corsage pin.

11   Set the tussie in a shallow vase or glass with some water until you give it away.

HOW TO DRY, STORE, AND USE LAVENDER

Lavender is the fragrant flower that keeps on giving! There are countless ways to use dried lavender, both as loose flower heads and as stems. This is how to harvest, dry, and store lavender for future use.

1. Harvest the lavender stalks.
Harvest lavender stalks in early morning (once the dew has dried) when the fully formed buds are closed and one or two flowers are just starting to bloom. Harvesting the stalks at this time will give the dried lavender the longest-lasting scent. Cut the longest stem that you can while leaving at least two or three sets of leaves on the plant to encourage more flowers stalks.

2. Dry the lavender.
Tie about 12 lavender stalks together with twine or rubber bands. I use rubber bands because they contract as the stalks dry. Hang the bundles up in a dry, protected area that has good air circulation. Good choices are a loft, a barn, an attic, or the shady side of a covered porch. Your lavender will be thoroughly dry in about 4 weeks.

3. Store the lavender.
Once they are dry, you can leave the stalks hanging until you use them. You could also remove the flower buds for tea, lavender bags, potpourri, or anything else that requires them to be loose. To remove them, place a bowl under the bunch and simply run your hands gently along the stalks. Store loose lavender buds in a box, paper bag, or jar.

HOW TO USE DRIED LAVENDER

Baked goods.
Add some authentic lavender flavor to cookies, cakes, scones, and bread.

Jams and jellies.
Fancy up your blackberry, blueberry, pear, peach, or strawberry jams and jellies by adding a little lavender.

Lemonade.
Yes, lavender lemonade is a thing.

Essential oils.
Lavender essential oil is used most widely for its calming effects on the mind and body.

Bathtub soak.
Relax, let the stress go, and soothe aching muscles by soaking in a tub with lavender essential oils and flower buds.

Body products.
Make a lavender body scrub. Then whip up some nourishing body butter to nourish your skin and relax the mind.

Candles.
Use lavender oil and dried lavender buds in your homemade candles. Then add the long stalks to the outside for embellishment.

Heating pads.
Fabric scraps, dried lavender, and rice do wonders for aching muscles and cramps.

Eye pillows.
Insomnia, stress, and headaches don't stand a chance against lavender.

Household cleaners.
Take advantage of lavender essential oil's natural antibacterial and deodorizing properties.

Wands.
Lavender wands can be used the same way as sachets—they're just fancier (and sometimes we want fancy).

Lavender water.
Use lavender water on acne, hair, and skin.

Linen water.
Freshen up pillows, bedding, or an entire a room.

Sachets.
Lavender sachets come in handy for drawers, closets, or wedding or shower favors—even as dryer bags!

Shampoo.
Remember the antibacterial and deodorizing properties?

Soap.
Lavender magically turns homemade soap into artisanal soap.

Loose-leaf tea.
Tea drinkers swear by lavender's soothing properties to help ward off headaches, anxiety, stomach upset, and sore joints.

Décor.
Make wreaths, hanging bundles, and potpourri for your home.

3

THE HANDCRAFTER'S HEIRLOOMS

---

*"I perhaps owe
having become a painter
to flowers."*

—Claude Monet

I don't think anyone would argue that the arts aren't a major component of the human experience. Art in any form is creative expression at its best, and handcrafting is one of my favorite art categories. Learning and practicing a craft or skill that produces something entirely new (entirely you) is incredibly rewarding.

Certainly, handcrafting has been with us since the beginning of the human race. But you may have noticed that we are currently enjoying the day of the DIY, and as a creative, handcrafting art lover, I'm in my element! This chapter will remind you that heirloom flowers are more than just a pretty face.

If you're a handcrafter, plant some heirloom flowers that go beyond the vase. From pressed flowers, botanical dyes, flower crowns, and floral paper, to candles, soap, beauty aids, décor, flower pounding, and bouquets—heirloom flowers can become your medium for artful expression.

I have to share with you one of my favorite quotes of all time:

Everyone must leave something behind when he dies, my grandfather said. A child or a book or a painting or a house or a wall built or a pair of shoes made. Or a garden planted. When people look at that tree or that flower you planted, you're there.

It doesn't matter what you do, he said, so long as you change something from the way it was before you touched it into something that's like you after you take your hands away.

The difference between the man who just cuts lawns and a real gardener is in the touching, he said. The lawn-cutter might just as well not have been there at all; the gardener will be there a lifetime.

—Ray Bradbury

Bradbury combines gardening, art, and crafting so beautifully. Don't his words just fill you up? I knew you'd understand.

CALENDULA
(CALENDULA OFFICINALIS)

Calendula is known as pot marigold, English marigold, and poet's marigold.

CALENDULA'S common names are pot marigold, English marigold, and poet's marigold. Its historical use in soups and stews gave calendula the nickname "pot" marigold. One can only surmise that Shakespeare's calendula tea recipe in his play *A Winter's Tale* earned it the "poet's" marigold moniker. Pot marigold (*Calendula*) and common marigold (*Tagetes*) are not the same genus, although they are in the same (sunflower/daisy) family. If you ever find yourself confused between the two, give the flower head a sniff. Calendula doesn't share the same pungent marigold scent of *Tagetes*. Their leaves will also tell the tale. Calendula leaves are ovate (egg-shaped), while *Tagetes* leaves are pinnate (divided).

Calendula is native to southern Europe and became a British garden mainstay by the fifteenth century. It's an incredibly versatile plant that's been used since ancient times for its medicinal properties. Because of calendula's antihemorrhagic and antiseptic value, it has been used on open wounds in the battlefield. In fact, Gertrude Jekyll grew calendula in abundance during World War II to send to the first aid medics for wound dressing. Among a variety of other things, it's been used to treat skin conditions and to detoxify the liver and gallbladder, and it has powerful anti-inflammatory properties. Calendula is still used today in natural remedies, both internally and as a main ingredient in salves and poultices.

You've probably already surmised that pot marigold is used in culinary dishes. Aside from stews and soups, it looks and tastes great in salads, as well as in egg and fish dishes.

All this and she makes a fabulous cutting flower too! Calendulas are long-blooming, hardy annuals that produce single and double gold, orange, cream, and yellow flower heads. Plants grow to 1 to 2½ feet tall. They may bloom through the summer if temperatures stay below 85°F. Where summers are hot (I'm looking at you, California), figure on getting only spring and fall blooms. However, in mild winter areas, she will flower from fall all the way until the next spring.

Calendula tolerates most soil as long as it's well draining.

Start seeds indoors 4 to 6 weeks before the last frost. Feel free to transplant hardened-off seedlings outdoors a couple of weeks before the frost date in your area has passed (calendulas can take it). Plant them 10 to 15 inches apart in full sun or part shade. You can also sow seeds directly into the garden bed in late fall for the earliest spring flowers.

She will tolerate most soils if the drainage is good. However, her dream soil is sandy loam if you're offering. Calendula appreciates a nutritious soil, so top-dress the bed with compost every now and again. But don't get all fertilizer happy or you'll sacrifice blooms. Water evenly and pinch off languishing flower heads to encourage a bushier plant and more flowers. Pot marigolds make terrific container plants.

Keep dried calendula petals around for crafting.

NOTE

Please seek proper guidance if you would like to use calendula as a medical treatment. Do not drink or eat calendula if you are pregnant.

ENGLISH LAVENDER
(*LAVANDULA ANGUSTIFOLIA*)

"English" lavender (*L. angustifolia*) is actually a native of the western Mediterranean and northern Spain.

BRITAIN was introduced to lavender via the Romans, who had long since been bathing with the aromatic plant. In fact, "lavender" is derived from the Latin word *lavare*, which means "to be washed." English lavender (*L. angustifolia*) is the species typically grown for crafting, eating, and as cut or dried flowers because it has the strongest fragrance. This is the type we're focusing on here. Other lavender species that are also grown for their scent—just less so—are French and Spanish lavenders. Both French and Spanish types are identified interchangeably as *L. dentata*, *L. stoechas*, and *L. lanata*.

As happens way too often in the plant world, the common names don't always ring true for the plant. Although it was dubbed "English" lavender, *L. angustifolia* is a native of the western Mediterranean and northern Spain. Lavender has been grown for centuries for its anti-inflammatory and antiseptic properties. Its perfume was used to disguise body and other unpleasant odors, and the flower stalks were kept for crafting, fragrance, and as a moth repellent.

She's as much of a workhorse today as she was in the past. English lavender attracts butterflies and bees; it is deer and rabbit resistant; it adds texture and scent to the cut flower bouquet; and it has endless uses for the handcrafter. Lavender is a shrublike, perennial evergreen plant that's hardy all the way to Zone 5.

Mature lavender plants are semiwoody in nature and the new growth is a soft and pliable gray-green. In the summer, tiny, fragrant lavender-blue flowers show up on spikes. Starting lavender from seed is difficult; it's much easier to propagate them from cuttings or purchase young starts from a nursery.

Plant lavender in full sun and average (not rich), well-draining soil. Soil type is flexible, but wet, heavy, clay soil is a death sentence. Soil that's on the alkaline side will enhance the fragrance of the lavender, and a sunny slope is the ideal situation for growing lavender plants.

When planting new lavender, dig a hole deep enough to just allow the top of the rootball to be flush with the ground. In other words, don't plant them too deeply. Newly planted lavender needs regular watering until the plants have become established. Once the plants are growing well, however, lavender can handle drought conditions and needs to be watered only after the soil is dry. In the early spring, trim the plants back by a third to encourage new growth.

- **'Hidcote'** has dark, purple-blue flowers and is highly fragrant; it grows 18 inches tall and wide.

- **'Munstead'** is excellent as a fresh-cut flower, as well as in dried bouquets; grows 18 inches tall and wide.

- **'Vera'** has deep lavender-blue flowers and is 36 to 48 inches tall and wide.

NOTE

Check out "How to Dry, Store, and Use Lavender" in Chapter 2.

Lavender has endless uses for the handcrafter.

GLOBE AMARANTH
(*GOMPHRENA GLOBOSA*)

Gomphrena globosa is native to Brazil.

Drying globe amaranth bundles

IN THE RECENT past, globe amaranth hasn't seemed as popular as many of the other cottage-garden heirlooms. They haven't been as cherished as some of the more bold and bountiful girls that make up the more popular crowd. But like everything else that falls out of favor, their time has come back around. Gardeners are sitting up and taking notice as they find them tucked inside arrangements from their local florists. Artisans are rediscovering the beauty they bring to crafts. Once again, the small girls with the textured personality are finding their place in the American garden.

Gomphrena is native to Brazil and made her way to Europe from India in 1714. Her superhero power is that she is one in a special group of flowers called "everlastings." She's a long-lasting cut flower that becomes a marvelous dried flower. In other words, her makeup today looks as good as it did the day she put it on three years ago. (Try that trick, Dahlia.)

Her cloverlike "flower head" is actually a bunch of colorful, papery bracts (modified leaves that look like petals), although if you look very closely, you will find some itty-bitty white or yellow flowers. The original globe amaranth color is magenta, but you'll now find them in pink, red, white, and lilac.

Globe amaranth is a prolific annual that grows to 24 to 30 inches tall and attracts a wide variety of butterflies. When it comes to soils, she's just about as accommodating as she can get. Average to poor soils are her wheelhouse. She laughs in the face of drought and says, "Bring it on!" to clay soils. *Gomphrena* blooms from early summer all the way to a hard frost. For a top performance, give her a well-draining soil and even watering.

I always advise starting *Gomphrena* seeds indoors 6 to 8 weeks before the last frost date. It takes a couple of months from seed to flower, so the jump start will bring the earliest blossoms. Soak the seeds for 24 hours before sowing them to bring a higher germination percentage. Plant them about ½ inch deep in a seed-starting medium. Transplant hardened-off seedlings to the garden after the last frost date. If you choose to sow the seeds directly into the garden bed, do so after the last frost date has passed and be generous with the seed. Because you won't be presoaking the seeds, the germination percentage will be lower. Maintenance while growing is simple: give the plants a little compost every now and again and pinch them back to encourage bushiness. You're going to be delighted that you planted her.

HONESTY

(*LUNARIA ANNUA*)

Lunaria annua represents honesty and sincerity.

HONESTY is native to the Balkans and southwest Asia and has naturalized in Europe and North America. *Lunaria annua* is also called silver dollar plant and moonwort. She's most commonly referred to as "honesty" courtesy of the Victorians. Victorians enjoyed expressing their feelings through flowers, creating the "language of flowers," for which every blossom had a meaning attached to it. *Lunaria annua* represents honesty and sincerity. The genus, *Lunaria*, was named for the flat, moon-shaped disks that contain the plant's

seeds. Honesty was a medieval garden favorite and peaked in popularity during the 1800s with the Victorians. By 1667, it was happily growing in the New England gardens of colonists.

Don't let the specific epithet (*annua*) confuse you: honesty is a biennial, not an annual. Her cheery single-petaled flowers, purply-pink, purple, or white, have a light, sweet scent. Flowers appear May to July. Honesty is an attractive plant with oval- to heart-shaped serrated leaves.

Honesty is an eager self-seeder.

Mid–late summer, the flowers give way to flat green seedpods. Once the seedpods turn brown, you can gently peel the brown layer away to reveal the silvery disk. The translucent seedpods are as charming as they are surprising, and middle-class Victorian ladies often made them an art—literally. They hand-painted miniature designs and scenes on the gossamer pods.

Beatrix Potter, beloved English writer, illustrator, and conservationist, enjoyed honesty as much as I do:

> *I went to see an old lady at Windermere,*
> *and impudently took a large basket and*
> *trowel with me. She had the most untidy*
> *overgrown garden I ever saw.*
> *I got nice things in handfuls without*
> *any shame. . . Stolen plants always grow.*
> *I stole some "honesty" yesterday, it was*
> *put to be burnt in a heap of garden refuse!*

Passalong plants, indeed.

Because honesty isn't a fan of transplanting, most people prefer to sow seeds directly outdoors rather than starting them indoors (she's a rather eager self-seeder). Plant seeds into the garden bed in late spring or early summer and they will form basal leaf rosettes; flower stalks will come up and flower the following spring. *Lunaria* is happy hanging out in well-draining, average to poor soil if it has moisture. Full sun is good, but they seem to be happiest in dappled shade. A beautiful specimen for a woodland garden setting.

The dried seedpods of *Lunaria* bring texture, interest, and beauty to dried flower arrangements. Harvest the pods for dried flower arrangements by removing the stalk once the pods begin to turn brown. Hang them upside down in a cool, dry, and well-ventilated area to finish drying completely. I suggest that you leave some on the plants, as well, for a beautiful and shimmering fall and winter garden display.

Please don't let the wait for the flowers and pods steer you away from planting *Lunaria*. You're going to be so pleased with yourself come early spring when they are blooming away and there's little else to offer color.

Translucent seedpods are perfect for dried arrangements.

Pressed flowers.

If you make a habit of pressing flower heads every so often, you'll soon have a wonderful collection to work with. Here are some ways to use pressed flowers.

- Press them between two pieces of framed glass. Hang it in the window to look like stained glass.
- Glue them to stock paper to make greeting cards or bookmarks.
- Make pressed-flower resin jewelry.
- Embellish a phone cover or clear switch plate.
- A little glue sealer and pressed flowers will create the classiest Easter eggs you've ever seen. Blow the eggs out and keep them forever.

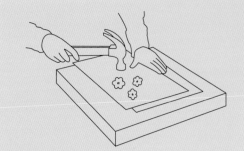

Flower pounding.

Flower pounding is basically smashing the flowers and/or stems to leave an imprint on fabric or paper. (It's prettier than it sounds.)

Get Your Garden Art On: Floral Craft Ideas

Tussie mussies.

Tussie mussies are small hand bouquets that are also known as nosegays. They are easy and adorable. We're hoping to bring them back for birthdays, anniversaries, Mother's Day, May Day, and any other day we can think of. Instructions for this are also in Chapter 2.

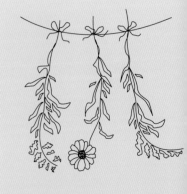

Dried flowers.

"Everlastings" such as statice, strawflower, or globe amaranth are sort of naturally dried flowers. You can also dry regular flowers, such as lavender, zinnia, hydrangea, roses, sunflowers, and chrysanthemums, for crafting by letting them dry naturally as they hang from their branches upside down. They can also be dried in the oven or with silica gel.

Natural flower dyes.

Heirloom flowers such as marigolds, dahlias, coreopsis, daylilies, hollyhocks,daffodils, cosmos, yarrow, and black-eyed Susan make wonderful botanical dyes for natural fibers such as wool, cotton, and silk.

Handmade floral paper.

This consists of blending shredded scrap paper into a pulp and adding flower petals. Each individual floral paper is always beautiful and unique.

Body scrubs, bath salts, and lotions.

Have a spa day in your own home with handmade body scrubs, bath salts, and lotions using flowers such as calendula, rose, lavender, and chamomile.

Home décor.

Make wreaths, hanging bundles, and potpourri for your home using dried or fresh flowers.

Candles.

Floral essential oils can be used in handmade candles. Pressed flowers can be used to embellish the outside.

Artisan soap.

Homemade artisanal soaps and heirloom flowers are a match made in heaven.

Flower crowns.

Once you've made one, you'll be hooked forever more. Flower crowns are simple to make and a joy to wear. Check out Chapter 2 for the instructions.

LOVE-IN-A-MIST

(*NIGELLA DAMASCENA*)

Nigella damascena takes 90 to 100 days to bloom. But she is so worth the wait.

NIGELLA DAMASCENA is one of my favorite heirloom plants of all time, and she happens to have some of the most entertaining nicknames, including love-in-a-mist, devil-in-a-bush, ragged lady, lady-in-a-bower, St. Katharine's flower, love-in-a-puzzle, Jack-in-the-green, and Jack-in-prison. *Nigella* is native to southern Europe and North Africa.

Nigella is *old*, folks. Theophrastus, the Greek philosopher and botanist, acknowledged the plant back in 300 BCE. England got its hands on *Nigella* and was cultivating it in 1570. Originally, it was used medicinally for digestive issues, and the seeds were used to flavor culinary dishes. By the end of the sixteenth century, plantsmen had created double-petaled varieties, and now we've got a pretty plant.

Love-in-a-mist is a unique-looking plant with erect, feathery foliage that gives the whole plant a misty appearance. There's also a lacy bract surrounding the delicate, blue, pink, white, or violet flowers like a collar.

The seedpods that follow the flowers are, perhaps, the plant's true treasure. They are balloon shaped and start out as a light green seed capsule. They eventually turn brown and have little horns on the top, giving them a rather devilish look (devil-in-a-bush). *N. damascena* makes a great cutting flower and the seedpods become beautiful everlastings. They add texture and interest to dried flower arrangements, wreaths, and flower crowns.

These hardy annuals survive almost any soil type but prefer sandy soils with good drainage and full sun. Seeds can also be started 4 to 6 weeks before the last frost indoors. However, *Nigella* has a long taproot and isn't thrilled with being transplanted. Better to sow the seeds directly into the garden bed in early spring. In mild winter climates, sow them into the garden bed in the fall for early spring blooms. The seedlings will pop up in 10 to 21 days. Plants grow 12 to 30 inches tall and bloom in the early summer. You can extend the flower show by succession planting, which in this case means starting a batch of seeds every 2 weeks, beginning in early spring to June.

Here's the part where I lecture you about having a little patience. If you don't have any, you'll have to borrow some, because love-in-a-mist takes her own sweet time blooming. Like 90 to 100 days of sweet time. Deadheading spent flowers will certainly bring more flowers. That said, don't forget to leave some on the plant so you can meet love-in-a-mist's alter ego, devil-in-a-bush. You'll want to collect these fabulous seedpods, trust me.

Nigella damascena is a must-have for the cottage garden. She doesn't have any particular pests or diseases to worry about. Although the plants are prolific self-seeders, they are easily pulled up should your garden suddenly feel overwhelmed by them. Heirloom varieties that are easy to find today include:

- **'Cambridge Blue'** has deep blue semidouble-petaled flowers.

- **'Miss Jekyll Alba'** has white semidouble-petaled flowers.

- **Miss Jekyll Blue'** has semidouble-petaled sky blue flowers.

Love-in-a-mist blooms in blue, pink, white, and violet.

The horned seedpods earned them the devil-in-a-bush moniker.

MARIGOLD

(*TAGETES ERECTA* AND *T. PATULA*)

All marigold species are easy-keepers and don't have a list of demands.

DESPITE their curious nicknames, both French (*T. patula*) and African (*T. erecta*) marigolds are originally from Mexico. *T. erecta* arrived in Spain in the early sixteenth century. They made their way to southern Europe and moved on to northern Africa, where they became completely smitten with the region and proceeded to naturalize themselves. They were dubbed "African marigolds" ever after.

T. patula caught a ride from Mexico to France and was introduced to England in 1853. As far as the English were concerned, these were French marigolds. In any case, both species reached Britain sometime during the sixteenth century, were embraced by the people, and planted far and wide. French marigolds grow 6 to 20 inches tall and the African marigolds grow 10 to 36 inches tall.

You may have heard about marigolds repelling nematodes (microscopic worms) in the soil, thereby protecting themselves and other plants from becoming a host to these parasites. The roots of both French and African species produce a chemical called alpha-terthienyl, which inhibits nematode eggs from hatching. French (*T. patula*) marigolds seem to perform exceptionally well in this function.

Tagetes blooms in yellow, orange, white, russet, mahogany, and bicolors.

Although millions of people plant marigolds alongside their vegetable crops to inhibit nematodes, there's another strategy that's more effective. A little research will convince you that planting the marigolds as a cover crop in the vegetable bed 2 months ahead of crop planting is the better strategy.

Marigolds are easy-keepers and have no true list of demands. They bloom their little heads off in full sun, but have no interest in sulking and won't withhold flowers in light shade. Marigold flowers come in yellow, orange, white, russet, mahogany, and bicolors. Their aromatic foliage has an interesting scent that is nothing at all like the sweet perfume of the rose or carnation. It can be quite pungent, but not necessarily unpleasant.

You can get a jump start on blossoms by starting marigolds indoors 6 to 8 weeks before the last frost. Once your local frost date has passed, you can simply sow seeds directly into the garden bed. Marigolds enjoy a loamy, well-drained soil but will tolerate almost any soil they sink their feet into. Give them a sunny garden position, as they can take the heat. But in order to survive extremely hot weather, the soil shouldn't be left to dry out.

You can fertilize marigolds lightly once or twice during the summer by watering them with a compost tea solution or other natural fertilizer. However, if you overdo it, you'll sacrifice blooms. I don't specifically fertilize my marigolds, per se, although I do add compost to the bed a couple of times a season. Deadheading blooms as they fade will keep the flowers coming all summer.

She may be common, but marigold is a treasure. Did I mention that her flowers are edible and they also make a wonderful botanical dye? Marigolds are nearly foolproof to grow, making them perfect for children as well as the beginning gardener.

Marigolds are at home in containers.

ROSE-OF-SHARON
(*HIBISCUS SYRIACUS*)

Hibiscus syriacus blooms in pink, white, or lilac with maroon centers.

OFTEN called "shrub althea," rose-of-Sharon is a hardy (Zones 5 to 9) deciduous shrub that grows up to become what is basically a small-trunked tree. In the eighteenth century, she was coined by Carolus Linnaeus "hibiscus Syria," as the handsome plant was thought to have originated in the Middle East. Actually, however, she's a native of India and East Asia. Rose-of-Sharon averages 8 to 10 feet tall at maturity and attracts butterflies and hummingbirds midsummer to fall.

Plant rose-of-Sharon in full sun to partial shade. Pay attention to the "partial" part. If she gets *too* much shade, she won't give up the flowers. Moist, well-draining soil is important to her. Add a light application of balanced, organic fertilizer in the spring. Because she blooms on new wood (and later than most), prune or shape rose-of-Sharon in early spring. Here's another plant that appreciates a little patience. She sleeps for quite a while during the off-season. Her leaves are lost in the fall and don't show up again until late spring. When the leaves do show up, they are attractive, three-lobed, and medium to dark green.

Heirloom *H. syriacus* has five-petaled, single blossoms in pink, white, or lilac with dark maroon centers. The individual flower lives are quite short—just a day or two. However, the blooms are so abundant that I doubt you'll notice. They are one of my favorite flowers to press. Rose-of-Sharon flowers are edible and can be used in salads, quiches, soups, and dips and steeped to make tea.

I've heard the whispers along the horticultural grapevine that there are those who despise the lovely rose-of-Sharon. I have asked for reasons but have yet to hear sensible answers to the distaste. Some claim that *H. syriacus* is an unattractive specimen come winter, but that's simply not enough to cancel *this* gardener's rose-of-Sharon fan card.

That said, I offer fair warning that rose-of-Sharon self-sows freely. This is a double-edged sword, because on one hand, you'll have no problem passing it on to another gardener. On the other hand, she is labeled as invasive in some areas.

This young rose-of-Sharon will quickly resemble a small-trunked tree.

STATICE

(*LIMONIUM SINUATUM* AND *L. PEREZII*)

Sea lavender (*Limonium perezii*)

STATICE was cultivated in the seventeenth century, both as a cut flower and as an herb for its astringent properties. Two heirloom species still grown today for cut flowers and crafting are *Limonium sinuatum* (common statice), a Mediterranean native, and *L. perezii* (sea lavender), a native of the Canary Islands. There are slight differences between the two species, the first being that *L. sinuatum* is an annual and *L. perezii* is a short-lived perennial (Zones 9 to 11) that's often grown as an annual. Sea lavender is a bit taller (3 feet) than the common statice (1½ to 2 feet).

They both thrive in average, well-draining soil in full sun. However, while sea lavender needs only moderate watering, common statice needs consistent moisture. Overwatering will make statice susceptible to root and crown rot. Think in terms of damp, not soggy, soil.

Sow statice seeds indoors 6 to 8 weeks before the last frost, covering them lightly with seed-starting medium or peat moss. Keep the seeds moist but not wet. Statice seeds can also be sown directly into the garden bed after the last frost date has passed. Germination can take up to 3 weeks, so be patient. The young plants should be 18 inches apart for good air circulation.

Plants produce dark green, wavy-leafed, basal rosettes that hug the ground. In summer to late fall, the papery, funnel-shaped blooms are borne horizontally at the end of tall, stiff, winged, and almost leafless flower stems. *L. sinuatum*'s flowers are purple, pink, lavender, rose, yellow, or creamy white, and *L. perezii*'s flowers are purple.

Statice can sit in a vase with no water and last forever.

Although statice hasn't enjoyed the same popularity as some of the antique cottage flowers in the recent past, I'm telling you they are worth a second look. Both *Limonium* species bring texture, color, and longevity to fresh-cut flower arrangements. Plus, once they have been dried, they earn their keep as everlastings for crafts such as dried arrangements and wreaths.

To harvest statice as an everlasting, when the flowers are about 75 percent open, cut a 12- to 18-inch flower stem off of the plant. Secure a few bunches at the bottom of the stems with a rubber band. Hang the bunches upside down in a cool, well-ventilated area out of direct sunlight. The flowers will continue to open as they dry. Statice will be completely dried and ready for craft use in about 2 weeks.

Cut statice from the plant when flowers are about 75 percent open. Flowers continue to open as they dry.

STRAWFLOWER

(BRACTEANTHA BRACTEATA OR XEROCHRYSUM BRACTEATUM OR HELICHRYSUM BRACTEATUM)

Harvest strawflowers when they are about halfway open. They will continue to open as they dry.

IS IT JUST ME? Why aren't people talking more about this fascinating heirloom flower? Just the fact that she belongs to the "everlasting" category makes strawflower a must-have in the heirloom or handcrafter's garden.

Everlastings are plants that have a papery texture, and they retain their shape and color long after all other flowers hit the compost pile. Everlastings enjoy two lives—the first in a cut flower arrangement, and the second in dried arrangements, wreaths, or other crafts for years ever after. It's a cool trick that only a handful of flowers can pull off. Having everlastings (or dried flowers) around the house means you're ready at a moment's notice to create decorations and gifts for the holidays.

Strawflowers, in particular, are *born* dried, which is hard to explain. Even as their juvenile petals being to unfurl, you can see and feel their crisp, papery texture. Flowers show up in an amazing variation of white, creams, yellows, orange, purples, and pinks. In 1803, French botanist Étienne Pierre Ventenat was the first to record strawflower as *Helichrysum bracteatum*. (Judging by the various names above, the rumors about botanists and their beer seem legit.)

Sow strawflower seeds indoors 6 to 8 weeks before the last frost in your area. Plant them in a seed-starting mix by pressing the seeds onto the surface of the mix. Don't cover the seeds, as they need light to germinate. Keep the soil moist until the seedlings show up. Harden off seedlings and then transplant them into the garden bed after the last frost date. If you want to plant seeds directly into the garden bed, make sure that you do so after the last frost date in your area.

Strawflowers are sun worshippers and need a place in the full sun. Like many flowers, they enjoy decent soil that's loamy in texture. That said, this is one flower that adapts just fine to poor soils. She is drought tolerant and needs water only sparingly. You can encourage a bushier plant with more blooms by pinching off the tips of the first growing stems. Do so early on at the beginning of the growing season; leave them alone after that and let the flowers show up. Deadheading (or cutting long flower stems for the vase) will also promote more flowers. Strawflower is an annual; however, she reseeds freely.

Harvest strawflowers when the blooms are about halfway open, as they will continue to open after they've been cut and are drying. Remove the leaves and bunch bottoms of stems together and secure with a rubber band. Then hang them upside down in a shaded, well-ventilated area for several weeks to dry. If you're planning on using them in a dried flower arrangement or a wreath, you may want to remove the stem and replace it with a floral wire. The dried stems become very brittle and break easily.

Strawflower is a must-have in every handcrafter's garden.

To wire the fresh cut strawflowers, first cut the stem from the flower. Using 22-gauge floral wire, cut a long piece off (stem length) and bend one end of it back, creating a small "U" shape. Go to the other end of the wire and stick it through the top of the strawflower head. Pull it through the head until the "U" is secured and buried in the flower. Once you've wired as many as you need, hang them upside down to dry completely.

If you've never grown strawflowers before, do so as soon as possible. The flowers are truly unique and I promise they'll make you giddy. They never get old (literally).

Also Very Vintage

Bearded iris

Aster

Daylily

There are many other heirloom flower species out there just waiting to be planted in your garden. Alas, there wasn't a reasonable way to include full profiles on every one of them. Through no fault of their own, this list drew the short stick. These well-loved plants also deserve a shout-out:

- **Aster** (*Aster* spp.): Purple, white, light blue, and pink asters make great cutting flowers.

- **Bearded iris** (*Iris germanica*): Bearded iris flowers are not only lovely but also extremely easy to grow. She offers a short window of bloom time, but is worth it in the perennial garden.

- **Canterbury bells** (*Campanula medium*): Also called bellflowers, *Campanulas* are essential to the cottage garden. They're great for the vase too.

- **Celosia** (*Celosia* spp.): Flower colors are seriously vibrant and come in plume or crested forms.

- **Chocolate daisy** (*Berlandiera lyrata*): This North American native smells like chocolate. You need it.

- **Columbine** (*Aquilegia* spp.): This North American native has both showy flowers and charming fernish leaves.

- **Crocus** (*Crocus* spp.): Crocus is a sight for sore eyes come the end of winter. It's one of the earliest of the spring bloomers.

- **Daylily** (*Hemerocallis* spp.): Although individual blooms last for only one day, the flower stalk produces many blooms during the season.

Japanese anemone

Lily-of-the-valley

Tulips

- **Four o'clocks** (*Mirabilis jalapa*): It's true, the flowers actually open at 4:00.

- **Geranium** (*Geranium pratense*): This is the perennial plant, not the annual known as pelargonium.

- **Hyacinth** (*Hyacinthus* spp.): An easy bulb to grow in shady woodland areas.

- **Japanese anemone** (*Anemone japonica*): Heirloom 'Honorine Jobert' is fabulous and still available today.

- **Lily-of-the-valley** (*Convallaria majalis*): A precious flower perfect in a tussie mussie or corsage.

- **Primrose** (*Primula vulgaris*): Blossoms show up like little hand bouquets in April and May and again in the fall.

- **Spiderwort** (*Tradescantia virginiana*): Have a soggy spot in the yard? Spiderwort understands and will give you no grief. This little darling actually thrives on neglect.

- **Tulip** (*Tulipa* spp.): The story goes that fortunes were made and ultimately destroyed due to a tulip virus. If you don't already know about tulip mania, you really must look it up. (Some believe that there's been a bit of embellishment thrown in through the years.)

And 'tis my faith, that every flower enjoys the air it breathes.

—William Wordsworth

HOW TO CREATE
A MARIGOLD-DYED SILK SCARF

Heirloom flowers that make great natural botanical dyes include marigold, daffodil, dark-colored zinnia, calendula, bee balm, dark-colored cosmos (*C. sulphureus*), dark-colored hollyhock, dark-colored dahlia, coreopsis (*C. tinctoria*), and daylilies (the spent flowers).

Botanical dyes have a hard time sticking to synthetic (man-made) fibers and work best on natural fibers that are either protein (animal) or cellulose (plant). Fibers produced by animals include wool, mohair, Angora, cashmere, alpaca, and silk. Cellulose fibers include bamboo, hemp, ramie, wood, muslin, linen, and cotton (although cotton usually has to have more preparation for the colors to adhere well).

Silk loves botanical dyes, so let's dye a silk fashion scarf with one of my favorite and versatile flowers—marigolds. Marigolds are wonderful because they produce vibrant yellows that are easily extracted and stick to fibers brilliantly (with or without the aid of a "mordant" like alum).

Creating a botanical dye involves collecting the plant parts (in this case, flower heads), extracting the color from them, and straining the plant parts out, leaving you with a natural dyebath. Once the dyebath is prepared, the fabric or fiber is added to the bath and allowed to simmer in order to take up the color.

Although it isn't necessary for us to pretreat our silk scarf with an alum mordant when using marigolds, I like to use it on everything I dye because it helps natural color adhere to the fabric/fiber and makes colors just a little brighter.

PREMORDANTING THE SILK SCARF

As far as how much alum and cream of tartar to use, I add 10 percent of the weight of my fiber or material. A silk scarf is so light that you'll only need about ½ teaspoon of alum. This simple mordant bath is often combined with cream of tartar to help brighten and clarify colors. Some dyers use it and some skip it, but I think it helps, so I keep it in the recipe. You can buy both alum and cream of tartar in the spice aisle in the grocery store.

MATERIALS

Stainless steel pot

Water source (kitchen sink)

Silk scarf

Stove

½ teaspoon alum (potassium alum sulfate)

¼ teaspoon cream of tartar (tartaric acid)

Measuring cup or small mixing container

Spoon or stirring stick

Tongs

Glass or ceramic bowl

1 Fill the pot with enough water to allow the scarf to float around freely. Add the scarf to the pot of water and place it on the stove. The reason we've added the scarf now is so it can slowly adjust to the rising temperature.

2 Place the alum and cream of tartar in the measuring cup and add a little warm water. Stir until they are dissolved and then pour the mixture into the pot on the stove. Turn the heat to medium. Bring it to a boil.

3 Once the water is boiling, immediately reduce the heat to just simmering. Let it simmer for about an hour.

4 Using your tongs, raise the scarf above the pot for a few moments, letting the water drain back into the bath. You can use it again later if you want to. Then place the scarf in a glass or ceramic (nonreactive) bowl to let it cool down for a bit so that you can handle it easily. Rinse the scarf with warm water.

5 Your scarf is now ready for the dyebath! No need to let it dry, just prepare the marigold dyebath below and you're ready to go.

MAKING A MARIGOLD DYEBATH

Step out into the garden and snap
off a bunch of marigold heads.
Another way to collect petals is
to deadhead faded blooms and
put them into a zip-top baggie
in the freezer until you've saved
up as much as you need. As far
as quantity needed, my general
guideline is to collect at least the
same weight in plant material
as I have fiber or fabric (1:1).

MATERIALS

Mordanted silk scarf

2 stainless steel pots and lids

Water source (kitchen sink)

Marigold petals or entire heads

Stove

Rubber bands (optional)

Mesh strainer

Stainless steel tongs

Glass or plastic bowl

1 tablespoon washing soda (optional;
find it on the laundry detergent aisle)

1 Make sure your silk scarf is thoroughly wet from the mordant bath.

2 Fill the first pot with enough water to allow the scarf to float about freely in the water, then remove the scarf. There's no need for more water than that. Add all the marigold petals (or the entire heads).

3 Put the lid on the pot, place on the stove, and heat the water slowly, bringing it to a gentle simmer (not boiling).

4 Optional Step: You can skip this part if you want to, but I want to tell you how I got the pattern on the scarf in the photo. Take the wet scarf and fold it in half. Fold it in half again. Now wrap sections of the scarf with the rubber bands (as many as you'd like), making the scarf into a bundle. Go on to step 5 whether you create a bundle or not.

5 Add the scarf. Slowly bring the water back to a gentle simmer, and simmer for about an hour. If you find that you can't resist peeking inside the pot (and really, who can?), please don't put your face over the pot while you lift the lid. Let the steam out for a few seconds before you peek, as steam can burn your face.

6 After an hour, place the mesh strainer over the second pot and drain the bath through the strainer so that the marigold petals become separated from the bathwater. Now place the dyebath (now in the second pot without the marigold petals) back on the stove. Once the bath is simmering again, add the silk scarf to the pot (either bundled or free-floating).

7 Let the scarf simmer in the dyebath for about 30 minutes.

8 Using the tongs, remove the scarf from the bath and place it into a bowl to cool down. Once it's cool enough to handle, rinse it off with fresh water from the sink.

9 If you left the scarf free-floating, you can hang it up to dry in a shaded, well-ventilated area that's out of direct sun. You now have a botanically dyed fashion scarf!

10 If you made a bundle with your scarf, after the bundle has been rinsed, add more rubber bands to the bundle.

11 Now, add the washing soda to the dyebath on the stove. Washing soda is a modifier and will change the color of the marigold bath slightly.

12 Add the now double-rubber-banded bundle to the dyebath. Let it simmer for about 20 minutes.

13 Use the tongs to remove the bundle and rinse it under running water in the sink. Once it's cool enough to handle, remove the rubber bands and rinse the entire scarf again.

14 Hang your one-of-a-kind artisan silk scarf to dry in a shaded, well-ventilated area that's out of direct sun.

HOW TO MAKE A ROSE AND LAVENDER BODY SCRUB

Among the limitless number of beauty potions created using heirloom flowers, body scrubs are one of my favorites.

MATERIALS

1½ cups granulated sugar

Large glass bowl

½ cup + 1 tablespoon coconut or olive oil

10–12 drops lavender essential oil

2 teaspoons dried lavender flower buds

Rose petals (one or two roses)

Spoon (or small scoop) for stirring and scooping

Airtight jar

1   Pour the sugar into a large bowl. Add the coconut or olive oil on top of the sugar.

2   Add the lavender essential oil drops on top of the coconut oil, then add the dried lavender buds to the bowl.

3   Add the rose petals by tearing them into a pleasing size. Drop the petals into the sugar mixture and stir until everything is well blended.

4   Scoop your body scrub into an airtight container. Scrubs with fresh ingredients such as flower petals will last in an airtight jar for about 2 weeks.

5   To use, apply a generous amount of scrub to wet skin and rub it onto your body in a circular motion. Rinse off.

4

COTTAGE
CLASSICS

---

*"To pick a flower
is so much more satisfying
than just observing it or photographing it. . . .
So, in later years, I have grown in
my garden as many flowers as possible
for children to pick."*

—Anne Scott-James

Most heirloom plants are, by their very nature, easygoing individuals. But perhaps you're new at gardening or maybe you'd like to dip your toes into the pond of heirloom flowers to test the waters. Or maybe you only have weekends available for gardening.

The heirloom plants in this last chapter are extra-hardy, easy to grow, and especially low maintenance, which makes for some incredibly popular ladies. These tough workhorses offer gorgeous heirloom flowers with minimum time investment.

Even if you're a seasoned gardener, the following flowers are well worth taking a look at. After all, I haven't met a gardener yet that prefers things that require mouth-to-mouth resuscitation on a weekly basis. Everybody appreciates a carefree girl!

Aside from their agreeable nature, these undemanding girls (like any other plant) show up in a variety of ways. Annuals produce leaves, flowers, and seeds, then they die all within the same growing season. Because they are in a big hurry to produce flowers, you get to enjoy a profusion of blooms the first year they are planted.

Perennial flowers are most certainly the backbone of the flower garden. They sometimes start their first year with a moderate amount of blooms. But perennials don't die in a single season. Depending on the species, they can live on for years, coming back bigger, stronger, and wider each year thereafter.

Biennials fill in the gap between annuals and perennials by germinating and producing their leaves (and strong roots) the first year they are planted. The payoff is in the second year, when they finally give up the goods (flowers). Some annual, perennial, and biennial heirlooms are enthusiastic re-seeders, thereby offering a leg up on the flower abundance for next year.

Balloon Flower
(*PLATYCODON GRANDIFLORUS*)

Balloon flower is a reliable and easy-to-grow perennial.

BALLOON FLOWER is one of my favorite perennials and I'm baffled as to why I don't see it in many gardens. She's as reliable as they come, easy to grow, and shows her good manners by not competing with other plants by spreading herself all over the garden.

Platycodon grandiflorus is native to China, Japan, Korea, and eastern Russia and is also called bellflower, Chinese bellflower, and Japanese bellflower. Balloon flower was introduced to Europe in 1782, but at some point after that the plant disappeared for a time. Scottish botanist Robert Fortune brought it back from China and reintroduced it to Britain in 1843.

The flower buds are entertaining from early summer to early fall as they puff up like a balloon until one day they burst open into adorable purple-blue stars. Plants are clump forming and grow 1 to 2 feet tall. The slender, light green leaves are placed alternately up the stem. Balloon flower is a perennial that's hardy in Zones 3 to 9. She enjoys rich, well-draining, loamy soil. Regular watering is fine, but don't overwater. She's rather drought-tolerant. Balloon flower is happy in full sun or part shade. In my Northern California garden, I've placed them in a spot that gets a half day of sun and dappled shade the rest of the time—they do fabulously.

Balloon flower can be grown from seed. However, the seed-grown heirloom *Platycodon grandiflorus* doesn't usually bloom the first year (although some of the newer varieties will). Start seed indoors in early spring in pots or cell packs. Press the seeds onto moist seed-starting medium. Don't cover them, as they

Flowers arrive looking like a little balloon.

need light to germinate. Seedlings will show up in 2 to 3 weeks. After hardening off seedlings, plant them outdoors 1 to 1½ feet apart.

For faster blooms, take a root cutting instead. Carefully dig down to the roots of an established plant and look for the place on the plant where a stem meets a root. Take a sharp knife and slice off the stem along with a 1-inch piece of root. Place the root/stem cutting into a container with a seed-starting medium or potting soil. Keep the soil moist and soon a baby balloon flower will take root. You can also dip the cutting into a rooting hormone before you plant it in the container.

Balloon flowers are not necessarily hungry plants. However, a sidedressing of compost a couple of times a year is appreciated. If the plants are kept deadheaded, you may find them reblooming in the fall.

Keep plants deadheaded and they may rebloom in the fall.

BLACK-EYED SUSAN

(*RUDBECKIA HIRTA* AND *R. FULGIDA*)

Black-eyed Susan is also known as brown-eyed Susan, brown Betty, and gloriosa daisy.

BLACK-EYED SUSANS are also called brown-eyed Susans, brown Betty, and gloriosa daisy. All these names are also used interchangeably between species *R. hirta* and *R. fulgida*, which are the *Rudbeckias* that we are most familiar with in our gardens. There are some differences between the two, but both are wonderful for many of the same reasons. For example, both species are hardy in Zones 3 to 9 and tolerate almost any soil if it's well draining. Both like full sun or light shade and need only moderate watering once established. These carefree plants are low maintenance and attract bees, butterflies, and birds to the garden. Both make a stunning display planted *en masse* and make great cut flowers for the vase. Both bloom summer to fall, respectively.

The genus was given to them by Swedish taxonomist Carolus Linnaeus, who named them for his botany teacher, Olof Rudbeck. The specific epithet, *hirta*, means "hairy," although the stems and leaves on *both* species are hairy. The species name *fulgida* means "shining" or "glistening."

R. hirta is a native of eastern and central North America that has naturalized throughout the United States and Canada. She's a biennial that was used as a medicinal herb for Native Americans. Her first growing year, the plant spends its time creating a basal rosette of medium green leaves. The flower stalks show up in the second year. That said, if they are planted early enough, you may get blooms the first year. *R. hirta*'s daisylike flowers are bright yellow with a center that is a firm, purple-brown cone. She's a free-seeding plant and is propagated that way.

Sow seeds directly into the garden 2 weeks before the last frost date in your area. Simply press them into the soil and don't cover them, as they need light to germinate. Start them indoors 6 to 8 weeks before the last frost to get a jump start on flowering.

R. fulgida is an eastern North American native. She's a long-lived perennial that produces gold-petaled flowers as opposed to yellow. Lower leaves form a rosette, while stem leaves are dark green, ovate, and alternate. Propagate these perennials by dividing the plants in the late winter or early spring. One of the most popular *R. fulgida* varieties today is called 'Goldstrum' (1937).

Rudbeckia makes a stunning display when planted *en masse*.

BLEEDING HEART

(*LAMPROCAPNOS SPECTABILIS* OR *DICENTRA SPECTABILIS*)

Bleeding heart is extra-charming in a woodland setting.

Bleeding heart flowers come in pink and white.

BLEEDING HEART is native to Siberia, Japan, Korea, and northern China. She was introduced in 1846 by Scottish botanist Robert Fortune, who acquired her from China. Her specific epithet, *spectabilis*, means "remarkable," "spectacular," or "showy." If you're interested in a laid-back plant that brings charming color to a shaded area, then bleeding heart is your girl.

Her most common name, bleeding heart, is most obviously due to her pink heart-shaped flowers with their white pistil "bleeding" down at the bottom. A couple of other common names are Dutchman's trousers and lady in the bath. Both seem a little obscure unless you turn the hearts upside down to get the visual. In any case, there isn't a more enchanting plant for a woodland setting.

Lamprocapnos spectabilis is an herbaceous perennial that's hardy in Zones 2 to 9. She thrives in dappled to medium shade that has moist and fertile soil. She grows 2 to 3 feet tall and wide and is an incredible easy-keeper. Come early April to mid-June, pink with white-pistiled flowers or pure white flowers arrive. Ten to twenty little hearts hang like cheerful charms on a slightly bowed, horizontal stem. The foliage on this plant is every bit as elegant as the flowers. The soft leaves are delicate, deeply lobed (almost lacy), and medium green. Unfortunately, the entire plant will have died back to the ground once midsummer arrives.

The easiest way to propagate bleeding heart is by dividing the plants after flowering in the summer, or by taking root cuttings in the winter. Bleeding heart can also be started by seed, but the seeds need a solid chilling period first. If you live in a mild winter area, plant them in a seed-starting medium and then cover them with plastic (or slide them into a zip-top baggie). Put the covered container into the freezer for 6 to 8 weeks. Remove them from the freezer and let them grow like any other germinating seeds. If you live in an area that has low winter temperatures, the seeds can get their cold period from the outdoors. Start them in a cold frame or directly in the garden bed. You can plant seeds directly into the garden in late fall or early winter.

Plant them 1½ to 2 feet apart where the soil is rich in organic matter (or add compost). They should have regular watering and light (if any) feeding. You may have noticed by now my penchant for all the Dr. Seussian plants. Whimsy is celebrated in my garden.

The foliage is every bit as elegant as the flowers.

NOTE

For all her playful charm, all parts of bleeding heart are poisonous.

Blue Flax

(*LINUM PERENNE*)

Flax's blue satin flowers last for one day. Never fear, as there are more right behind to take their place.

FLAX is an ancient, European native that's been cultivated to make linen cloth and extract flaxseed oil by early Mesopotamians, Egyptians, Greeks, Romans, Chinese, and more. People found a way to use every part of blue flax in their everyday lives. Various Native American peoples, for instance, found it useful for making rope and cordage, mats, baskets, fishing nets, and snowshoes. Oil could be extracted from the seeds; seeds could be roasted for eating or crushed to make meal. Flax was also used medicinally for colds, coughs, and general lung issues, as well as for creating poultices to reduce swelling.

Today we enjoy perennial blue flax as the gorgeous garden plant that she is. In case you were wondering, the flax plant that's commercially grown for linseed oil and to create linen items such as table linen and bedding is *L. perenne*'s annual relative, *Linum usitatissimum*, or common flax.

Blue flax's saucer-shaped flowers are a vivid sky-blue and absolutely stunning in the garden. Spring through midsummer, five-petaled flowers are born on 2-foot-tall stems and open just before dawn. The little satiny flowers last only one day, but there are many more to take their place throughout the season, as blue flax is a long-season bloomer.

The plant's gray-green, fernish foliage is attractive and adds texture to the garden. Plants need to be situated in full sun or you won't have any blooms. As long as the soil is well draining, blue flax makes herself right at home in poor, dry, or average soils; you'll have a hard time getting her to winter over if the soil is sopping and heavy.

Most people sow seeds directly in the garden after the last frost date, or indoors 4 weeks before the last frost date. However, if you want to encourage flowering the first year, I would plant the seeds in situ during the fall for spring blooms. Cover seeds with ⅛ inch of soil or seed-starting medium. Keep the seeds moist until germination. Blue flax is a short-lived perennial that's hardy in Zones 4 to 9. She self-seeds readily, but not aggressively so. Once she's done flowering for the season, you can trim the plant down for a tidy look, but I like to leave her as nature intended so she can reseed.

Linum perenne is the perennial blue flax.

NOTE

Please don't eat blue flax seeds unless you are guided by a professional. The raw seeds contain cyanide. Cooking the seeds does make them edible, but this book doesn't go into the correct way to prepare them.

CLEMATIS

(*CLEMATIS* SPP.)

Clematis likes her face in the sun and her feet in the shade.

CLEMATIS is native to northern Iran, Afghanistan, Lebanon, the Caucasus, southeast Britain, Asia, and Europe. In the late 1650s, *C. viticella*, a southern Europe native, was introduced to Britain. Once the Chinese species also made their way there, the larger flowered clematis hybrids were created. She's been nicknamed old man's beard, grandfather's whiskers, leather flower, and virgin's bower.

Today, there's something to the tune of 300 clematis species, not to mention the hundreds of varieties within those species. The flowers come in a wide range of shapes, sizes, and forms, from the spectacular to the subtle, and in every color you can think of. There are deciduous and evergreen clematis, vining and bush clematis—a little something for everybody. Many of them, thankfully, are heirlooms or heirloom-hybrids, if you prefer.

Cuttings are the easiest way to propagate clematis.

Clematis vines are truly easy to grow, but like hydrangeas, it's the pruning that can be confusing. The question is whether you should or shouldn't prune (or if you should—*then when?*). The answer depends on the type of clematis you have. The general approach is this: early-flowering types do not require pruning and can mostly be left to their own devices other than to trim back a robust plant or to untangle vines. Large-flowered, early-summer blooming types, which bloom on last season's wood, should be pruned lightly for structure while they are dormant. Late-flowering types, which bloom on new growth, can be pruned back to a pair of buds when they are deeply dormant. The takeaway here is that you should know which clematis species you've planted.

Some fabulous heirloom varieties include:

- **C. 'Elsa Späth'** (1891) has rich blue flowers with red anthers. Early-blooming, large-flowered clematis.

- **'Durandii Clematis' C. × *durandii*** (1870) has periwinkle flowers with butter-yellow centers.

- **'Jackman's Clematis' C. *jackmanii*** (1862) is a prolific, late-blooming, large-flowered clematis with violet-blue flowers.

- **'Madame Julia Correvon' C. *viticella*** (1900) has small, wine-red flowers in late summer to early fall. Late-flowering clematis.

Clematis enjoys life best where she can put her face in the sun and her roots in the shade. Fertile, well-draining soil is optimal. Plant her a bit on the deep side to help protect the roots against a fungus called clematis wilt. Water deeply and regularly. Fertilize once a year with a balanced organic fertilizer. Be sure to go light on the nitrogen. Since it takes 1 to 3 years for clematis seeds to germinate, the best way to propagate more is by taking cuttings and rooting them.

Clematis needs a support positioned next to it, such as a trellis, fence, or post, in order to climb. Netting placed on these structures will help the vines tremendously. Twiners use their leaves like tendrils to wrap themselves around string, wire, and other plants or leaves. So, ideally, you want to have a thin support for them to twist around.

A Plethora of Pollinators

Heirloom flowers are the superheroes of the natural pollinator world! Your heirlooms are loaded with what a bee wants, and what a bee needs. Namely, pollen and nectar. Pollinators, we've got your busy little backs.

(Apologies to Christina Aguilera for taking liberties with song lyrics.)

CORNFLOWER

(CENTAUREA CYANUS)

Cornflower is also called bachelor's button and bluebottle.

NATIVE to Europe and Asia, *Centaurea* has been cultivated for centuries, making her way to America in the 1600s. True blue flowers are scarce in the flower world, therefore, we tend to celebrate the plants that offer it up so freely. Cornflower is also known as bachelor's button and bluebottle (or blew-bottle).

So charming are the intensely blue flowers that Beatrix Potter made sure that the mayor's waistcoat was embroidered with them in her 1903 children's book, *The Tailor of Gloucester*. The Egyptian boy king, Tutankhamun, was buried in a wreath that included cornflowers (1327 BCE), although it's said to be *C. depressa*, not *C. cyanus*. Anyway, it's clear that humans had a big interest in *Centaurea* early on.

Cornflowers are hardy annuals that are effortless to grow. They are sun worshippers that tolerate poor and dry soils, grow 1 to 3 feet tall, and have branched stems with gray-green, lance-shaped leaves. The 1½-inch flowers show up in blue, purple, pink, and white in May through July. They make great cut flowers for the vase and can live their second lives as dried flowers for crafting. Planting them near yellow flowers such as calendulas or daylilies makes for a stunning garden display.

In cold winter areas, wait until after the last frost to sow seeds directly into the garden. Cover them with ½ inch of soil and space them 2 inches apart. When seedlings have their first set of true leaves, thin them to 6 to 12 inches apart. In areas with mild winters, cornflower seeds can be planted directly into the garden in fall for spring blooms. You can also start seeds indoors 4 to 6 weeks before the last frost. However, cornflowers are less than thrilled with being transplanted, so handle seedlings carefully when moving them into the garden bed. It bears mentioning that cornflowers self-sow readily.

Cornflowers appreciate regular watering, but they don't need much. Fertilizing is much the same way. However, if you feel the urge to fertilize, do so using a balanced fertilizer in the spring while the plants are still young. Deadheading flowers will encourage more blossoms to show up.

Heirloom cornflowers available today include:

- **'Blue Boy'** appeared during the seventeenth century, when Europe gave us these 2- to 3-foot-tall, brilliant blue boys.

- **'Jubilee Gem'** (1937) is an heirloom that is bright blue and double-flowered.

- **'Red Boy'** (1942) is a "newer" antique cultivar that's 2 feet tall and not true red, but more of a rose-red.

Cornflowers make excellent cut flowers for bouquets.

NOTE

Pretty is as pretty does. Cornflowers are considered invasive in some states.

Cornflowers dry beautifully.

Cosmos

(*COSMOS BIPINNATUS* AND *C. SULPHUREUS*)

Cosmos is the late-summer workhorse of the garden.

Cosmos thrives on a little bit of neglect.

ALSO KNOWN AS Mexican aster, *Cosmos bipinnatus* is native to Mexico and the southwestern United States and made its way to Britain in 1799. Butterflies are big fans of cosmos, and we are too. She's one of the easiest annuals to grow and a reliable workhorse in the late-summer garden.

Plant cosmos seeds directly into the garden in the late spring after the last frost date. Sprinkle a little soil over them so they are barely covered. They can also be started indoors 4 to 6 weeks before the last frost. Don't jump the gun and start them any earlier indoors, as the plants quickly become leggy. They are fast germinators and the seedlings pop up in 5 to 10 days.

Cosmos likes to set up camp in a sunny spot with well-draining but average soil. After that, please do your best to ignore them. By "ignore," I mean you should actually neglect the little darlings. Regular watering is fine, but don't overwater them, and whatever you do, don't overfeed them. In fact, when it comes to cosmos, step away from the fertilizer or you'll end up with a lot of green stuff while sacrificing the blooms.

Cosmos bipinnatus grows 3 to 4 feet tall. They are airy plants with medium-green, feathery foliage that makes a showy backdrop for the daisylike flowers that appear midsummer through fall. The 3- to 4-inch, saucer-shaped blooms pale pink, rose pink, or white with yellow centers. In excessively hot areas, the flowers might get a later start or slow down bloom production. If you thought neglecting them was tough love, watch this. When those first, hopeful flower buds show up on the plants, I want you to pinch them off. I realize that this sounds like a cruel pastime, but I assure you that you'll have bushier plants that produce more flowers than they would have if you hadn't pulled your big-girl panties on and did what needed to be done.

C. sulphureus, or yellow cosmos, was introduced in 1896 and is also a native of Mexico. This cosmos species is shorter than *C. bipinnatus* and grows 1 to 3 feet tall. The foliage is coarser (marigold-like) and the 2- to 3-inch flowers are gold, yellow, or orange. Yellow cosmos has a long blooming time from May to November. Both species make great cut flowers.

Some of my favorite cosmos are:

- **'Sea Shells'** has fluted, tube-shaped petals in shell pink, dark rose, and white.

- **'Sensation Mix'** flowers are light pink, rose, crimson, and white.

Garden Party Essentials

Now that you have a gorgeous garden filled with heirloom flowers, you simply must share it with the world and host a garden party! Invite friends and family into your garden to celebrate a birthday party, bridal or baby shower, special anniversary, or wedding. Or simply try something new and swap the barbecue flip-flops and tank tops for the summer hats and linen napkins of a slightly fancier affair.

Decorations.

Garden party decorations marry the formal, floral, and relaxing outdoors. Your blooming garden will do most of the heavy lifting as far as party decorations go.

- Hang bistro lights outdoors during an early evening event.

- Hang a chandelier outside over a table, maybe in a portico or on a tree branch. Weave greenery through it.

- Cut flowers in a vase on every table are a must.

- You could use floral-patterned paper plates and napkins. Or . . .

- You could break out the real stuff! Real plates, real silverware, and cloth napkins are appropriate for this event. By the way, formal garden parties always have "real" everything.

- Plates and napkins should match for a formal party. Mixed patterns work best for a more casual event.

Food.

All food served should look as lovely as it tastes. Break out your inner little girl—it's all about beauty.

- Appetizers should be light.
- Finger (tea) sandwiches, croissants, and pinwheels are appropriate lunch items.
- Skewered food makes it easy to nibble while wandering the garden.
- Fruit and salads can be served in individual plastic cups or goblets for easy eating and mingling.

Beverages.

Skip the colas this time.

- Serve (pink) lemonade, iced tea, raspberry punch, or perhaps berry smoothies.
- Floral cocktails and mocktails are most welcome at garden parties. (See "Drink Recipes.")

Dessert.

Never skip serving dessert at a garden party.

- Consider trifles, tartlets, strawberry shortbread, or English pudding.
- Fruit cups with real whipped cream and a ladyfinger cookie tucked into them are a simple dessert option.

Garden party favors.

Favors aren't necessary and are often unexpected. They're simply a delightful surprise for your garden party guests.

- Serve dessert in real teacups (guests take the teacup home).
- Plant individual small potted flowers, herbs, or succulents.
- Fill small sachets with flower seeds.
- Rewrap chocolate bars with beautiful floral paper.

HOW TO MAKE FROZEN FLOWER ICE CUBES

Flowers suspended in ice are simple and beautiful—a must-have for the garden party. Go all out and buy trays that make oversized, perfectly square ice cubes. They turn out so fancy (and last longer in the glass).

MATERIALS

Ice cube trays (I like the silicone types)

Distilled water (boiled and cooled)

Edible flowers from organically grown plants (we don't want to use flowers that have been sprayed with chemicals)

1 In order to make the flowers look like they are suspended inside the ice cubes, you need to create them in layers. Start by filling your ice trays about one-fourth of the way with water. To make the first layer of flowers, place them so they are facing down inside the tray. Freeze the trays.

2 Once that first layer is frozen, add more water to fill the cubes about halfway. Freeze the tray.

3 When that layer is frozen, fill the cubes the rest of the way up and add flowers facing up this time. Freeze the tray.

TIP

Boiling the water removes the air bubbles and gases, producing clearer ice cubes. If you were hoping for crystal clear ice cubes like those served in upscale bars, I'm going to tell you the cold, hard truth. You're not getting those at home. Those diamond-shiny bad boys are produced slowly by a special (expensive) ice machine and then someone hand cuts them individually. You don't need that. You've got orthodontist bills to pay and a party to set up.

DAFFODIL
(*NARCISSUS* SPP.)

Heirloom daffs come in white, yellow, pink, orange, and bicolors.

Yellow daffodils yield a lovely yellow natural dye.

DAFFODILS are extremely old and were first mentioned by the ancient Greek philosopher Theophrastus, who described *N. poeticus* 'Pheasant's Eye' in his botanical writings in 320 BCE. The Greeks and Egyptians cultivated them first, and daffodils made their way to English gardens by the 1200s.

These European and North African natives are trouble-free perennial plants and a favorite among gardeners. Once planted, daffodils naturalize into the landscape and bloom forever and ever. Seriously, the daffs that you plant today are the very same ones that your great-great-grandchildren will enjoy many years from now. They're deer-, rabbit-, and gopher-proof, as narcissus is poisonous and animals are smart like that. A lovely yellow dye can be extracted from the yellow daffodils, by the way.

Daffodils do well in areas that have full sun to light shade. In the fall, plant bulbs (point up) twice as deep as the bulb in loamy, well-draining soil. In other words, if your bulb is 3 inches tall, dig a hole that is 9 inches deep so that the bulb sits 6 inches under the ground. Bulbs need to have a chilling period of 12 to 16 weeks (at 40°F or lower). Usually their cold temperature exposure will come from the winter months spent underground, but for places that don't have cold winters, they may need to be artificially cooled in a refrigerator or by other means.

After planting, cover the bulbs with soil, water well, and then add a mulch such as chopped leaves or pine bark on top of them for protection. Of course, this is mostly important for zones that have extremely low winter temperatures. Heirloom daffodils come in white, yellows, pinks, oranges, and bicolors. The flowers have six outer petals (perianth) and a cuplike petal structure (corona) at the center. Believe me when I say that they are a sight for sore eyes when the daffs push up through the ground in late winter or early spring.

Instead of cutting off the green leaves after the flowers are spent, let the foliage die back naturally. The nutrients from the leaves are absorbed by the bulb, which allows it to come back the following year. After several years, the bulbs can be dug up in the fall, divided, and replanted.

Some antique daffodil favorites still around today include:

- **'Avalanche'** (1906) produces fragrant flowers that boast 15 to 20 blooms per stem.

- **'Butter and Eggs'** produces gorgeous double yellow flowers.

- **'Campernelle'** *N. × odorus* (1601) produces fragrant, early blossoms.

- **'Double Pheasant's Eye'** *N. plenus* (1861) produces a sweetly scented, double white perianth with a frilled yellow center with a red rim.

- **'Pheasant's Eye'** *N. poeticus* var. *recurvus* (1850) is a cultivar related to the original *N. poeticus*; produces fragrant, star-shaped, white petals with a yellow, red-edged cup with a green eye.

ECHINACEA
(*ECHINACEA PURPUREA*)

Echinacea is also known as purple coneflower.

ECHINACEA, commonly known as purple coneflower, is a native to North America that can be grown almost anywhere in the United States. This lovely wildflower attracts bees, butterflies, and birds and is just about as trouble-free as they come. *Echinacea* comes from the Greek *echinos*, meaning "hedgehog," which aptly describes the protruding cone at the center of the flower. *E. purpurea* was discovered in 1699, and in 1753, Swedish botanist Carolus Linnaeus classified them as *Rudbeckia purpurea*. When *Rudbeckia purpurea* was separated from the genus *Rudbeckia* in 1794, eighteenth-century German botanist Conrad Moench gave it the genus *Echinacea*.

All parts of *Echinacea* (flowers, leaves, stems, and roots) have been used both historically and today as herbal medicine. Aside from boosting the immune system, the plant has been touted as a treatment for infections, sore throats, coughs, fevers, colds, and flus. Although Western medicine has given it mixed reviews, some swear by the plant's healing properties.

Purple coneflower is a perennial that's hardy in Zones 3 to 8. In midsummer to early fall, she produces 4-inch, rosy-purple blooms on 2- to 4-foot-tall stems. Echinacea is drought-tolerant once established, but is at her best with moderate watering. She enjoys full sun and hot temperatures. Fertile soil is optimal, but she's a tough gal that will make the most out of any soil type if it's well draining. Plants are 2 to 4 feet tall with dark green, 3- to 4-inch lance-shaped, bristly basal leaves. Plant *Echinacea en masse* for the best visual effect. Don't worry about deadheading the spent blooms. In fact, if you let them stay, you can watch birds feast on the spiky seedheads.

Seeds can be directly sown into the garden in the early spring. Plant them ¼ inch deep, and after they germinate, thin the seedlings to 18 inches apart. You can also propagate them by division in the spring or take root cuttings during the winter.

Purple coneflower makes a wonderful cut flower for the vase. Even without the petals, the seedhead itself adds texture and interest to bouquets and arrangements.

Purple coneflowers are easy to grow and make wonderful cut flowers.

FORGET-ME-NOT

(*MYOSOTIS SYLVATICA*)

Myosotis in Greek means "mouse's ears."

THERE ARE quite a few stories describing how forget-me-not acquired her name. In one version, a young knight was picking the vivid blue flowers along a riverbank for his ladylove. The poor guy may have been a romantic, but he was also short on balance—he slipped into the strong current of the river (his armor probably didn't help). As he was swept away, he tossed the tiny flowers to his love, who was still standing on shore, and called out, "Forget me not!" There are other stories, of course. But I think that knights, armor, and tragic love might be the best way to come by a name.

This European native is a low-growing biennial that reaches about 1 foot tall and 2 feet wide. The hairy plant's lower leaves form a basal rosette, while oval and lance-shaped leaves alternate up the stems. Clusters of ¼-inch, true blue flowers with yellow eyes bloom in early spring to early summer when the soil is warm and the air is cool.

If you can't get enough blue in your garden (and really, who can?), then you must have *Myosotis sylvatica*. Forget-me-nots are prolific self-seeders, which goes to show you how determined she is not to let you forget. Once you've planted her, forever in your garden she will be. She likes shade or part shade and organically rich and moist soil. *Myosotis* in Greek means "mouse's ears," referring to the shape of the leaves. The specific epithet, *sylvatica*, means "forest-loving" or "growing in the woods." Forget-me-nots are especially happy in naturally damp places, such as near ponds or streams. *M. sylvatica* is hardy in Zones 3 to 9 and makes an excellent groundcover.

They are best propagated by seed. In mild winter areas, plant the seeds directly into the garden during the fall for spring flowers. In cold winter areas, they can be directly seeded a few weeks before the last frost, just before spring. To get a jump on the season, seeds can also be started indoors 8 to 10 weeks before the last frost.

Forget-me-nots bring the much-desired blue to the garden.

NOTE

In some regions,
Myosotis sylvatica
is too much of a good thing.
In other words, where
she's invasive, she's
a bad thing.

KISS-ME-OVER-THE-GARDEN-GATE

(PERSICARIA ORIENTALIS OR POLYGONUM ORIENTALE)

Kiss-me-over-the-garden-gate blooms in bright pink, light pink, or fuchsia.

PERSICARIA ORIENTALIS has collected a bucket of fun names over the years. Aside from kiss-me-over-the-garden-gate (my hands-down favorite name), there's prince's plume, prince's feather, princess feather, and ladyfingers. This hardy annual is native to Asia and completely owns the look with her exotic, catkin-like flowers.

Persicaria orientalis is an enthusiastic reseeder.

I find her common name alone completely irresistible. That said, *Persicaria* is considered an invasive plant species in some parts of the country. Please do your research to make sure this isn't the case in your neck of the woods before you plant her.

She's a handsome plant that grows to 6 to 9 feet tall with light, medium, or variegated green, heart-shaped leaves. Bright pink, light pink, and fuchsia draping tassels show up midsummer to fall. The tassels wave in a slight breeze and their light fragrance perfumes the air.

For the earliest blooms, start them indoors a whopping 14 to 16 weeks before the last frost date. Cover the seeds with about ¼ inch of seed-starting medium. *Persicaria* seeds have a flirty habit of taking anywhere from 1 week to 1 month to germinate. Giving the seeds a prechill in the refrigerator can help speed things along. To prechill seeds, use plastic wrap to cover the container of planted seeds. Place them in the refrigerator for several weeks.

The seeds can also be started outdoors on a cold frame in the early spring or sown directly into the garden. Be forewarned: she's an aggressive reseeder. So, once you've had her, you're pretty much married to her (unless she isn't happy at your house). But hey, you're in it for the long haul anyway, because she takes about 4½ months from seed to bloom.

Kiss-me-over-the-garden-gate likes full sun (or light shade if you must) and moist, well-draining soil. Average watering is all that's necessary once she's actively growing, so don't overwater. *Persicaria* is not a fussy girl, and although the seeds need a little coaxing, the plants thrive on near neglect. Bees and butterflies are smitten with her charm. The blooms make lovely and interesting cut flowers and are useful later as dried flowers for crafting.

LOVE-LIES-BLEEDING

(AMARANTHUS CAUDATUS)

Love-lies-bleeding is also called tassel flower and velvet flower.

I MET LOVE-LIES-BLEEDING for the first time in real life about sixteen years ago. She was huge and all draped about our community garden pathways. As I walked among the blood-red flower tassels, I wondered why I hadn't run into her before. Was she odd-looking? For sure. Gaudy? Probably. Stunningly dramatic? Always. I couldn't wait to have her hanging around my place. Drama (like whimsy) has an open invitation to my garden.

Native to Africa, India, and Peru, this ancient grain seemed to be on people's radar from the beginning. Seeds of amaranth species from 10,000 years ago have been discovered, as amaranth was a food staple for the Aztecs. Amaranth symbolized immortal life to the ancient Greeks, who adorned their temples and tombs with amaranth images. It was during the sixteenth century that *A. caudatus* became popular as an ornamental, and in 1810 it became available commercially. The Victorians were incredibly fond of it, and the varieties 'Green Thumb' and 'Viridis' became available during that time. Both had green flower tassels.

Love-lies-bleeding, also called tassel flower and velvet flower, is a tender annual and the first hard frost will bring her to her knees. The genus name *Amaranthus* translates to "never waxing old," referring to its dried flower qualities. The plant grows 3 to 8 feet tall and produces 2-foot-long flowers that hang like blood-red chenille. Occasionally, the plants will need staking. The lime-green, 6-inch-long oval leaves show off the dangling, crimson tassels to perfection.

Sow seeds directly into the garden after the last frost date has passed. Seeds can also be started indoors 4 to 6 weeks before the last frost. They germinate so easily that you might think it doesn't makes sense to take the extra steps to grow them indoors first. But it does take 60 to 70 days for the ropy flower tassels to show up, so getting a jump on germination means earlier flowers.

Plant hardened-off seedlings (or thin direct-seeded plants) 18 to 24 inches apart. Love-lies-bleeding grows just fine in average soils, but it thrives in organically rich ones. Although she doesn't need fertilizer, she wouldn't mind some aged compost thrown at her feet a few times a season. She's a hot weather lover, but needs even watering to keep the flowers fresh looking. Amaranths are wonderful as cut flowers in the vase and later as dried flowers for crafts. In the garden, planted *en masse*, she makes for a striking display.

Amaranthus caudatus dries beautifully.

Morning Glory

(*IPOMOEA* SPP.)

Ipomoea tricolor 'Heavenly Blue'

THESE WORLD-CLASS travelers are native to warm regions all over the world and first made their way to Britain via John Goodyer. Both *Ipomoea purpurea* (by way of Italy) and *I. tricolor* (by way of Spain) showed up in Britain at about the same time in 1621. *Ipomoea* eventually made her way to America in 1783. Neither species was met with open arms, however, as bindweed (*Convolvulus arvensis*) was making a complete nuisance of herself in gardens everywhere. Because morning glories look like they could be bindweed's big sister, you could hardly blame them for thinking *Ipomoea* would have the same cutthroat attitude.

The truth is that while they may resemble each other, morning glories are generally much better behaved. It's worth mentioning that morning glories and bindweed will not cross-pollinate, so don't let that keep you up at night.

NOTE

In some areas, morning glories are so prolific that they are considered a nuisance.

The popular *I. tricolor* 'Heavenly Blue' that we see today was derived from a very old heavenly blue that bloomed very late in the season. Then, a Colorado gardener named Clarke came across a mutated version of the plant that was an early-season bloomer of profuse, larger blossoms. Clarke offered some of the seeds to Dutch wholesaler Sluice & Groot, and in 1931 'Clarke's Heavenly Blue' became commercially available. *I. alba,* or moonflower, has a jasmine fragrance and was once popular in Victorian white evening gardens. Evening or night gardens were fashionable at the time because ladies were able to stroll through the gardens without exposing their skin to the sun.

Historically, morning glories were also used for religious ceremonies in Mexican culture to "commune with the gods" as officiants went into a dreamlike state after eating the seeds. The plants were also used by witches to cast spells on people. None of this will come as any surprise to you once you realize that the seeds contain d-lysergic acid amide (LSA), a compound similar to LSD. Ingesting them causes hallucinations. (For the record: Do *not* eat morning glory seeds. They are poisonous and cause a lot of other horrible things too.)

Technically, *Ipomoeas* are perennial plants, but only in the warmest regions. Almost everywhere else they are treated as annuals and die with the first hard frost. Morning glories like to be planted in full sun with some afternoon shade. They like average and well-draining soils. Rich soils will yield lots of foliage and very few flowers.

Free-Seeding Morning Glories

Nick (file) the seed coats and soak them overnight in some water. Sow seeds directly in early spring 2 weeks after the last frost date. Cover them with ½ inch of soil. You want to plant the seeds when the soil is consistently warm. Be sure to plant these vigorous climbers next to a trellis, fence, or another climbing support. Morning glories are free-seeding, so you'll have them every year thereafter.

You could sow them indoors several weeks before the last frost date, but most people don't bother because the flowers won't show up until mid- to late summer anyway. Try some of these old-timers in your garden:

- *I. alba* '**Moonflower**' has white flowers that open at dusk and have a jasmine scent on 30-foot vines.

- *I. purpurea* '**Grandpa Ott's**' has deep purple flowers with a crimson star at the throat on 15-foot vines.

- *I. tricolor* '**Heavenly Blue**' has sky-blue flowers with white throats and a touch of yellow on 15-foot vines.

- *Ipomoea × multifida* '**Cardinal Climber**' ('**Hearts & Honey**') (1880s) has cardinal red flowers on 20-foot vines.

I. purpurea 'Grandpa Otts'

PELARGONIUM
(*PELARGONIUM* SPP.)

What most people refer to as "geraniums" are technically pelargoniums.

WHAT MOST PEOPLE and garden centers refer to as "geraniums" are not true geraniums at all. They are technically pelargoniums. The true geranium is a different plant, commonly called a cranesbill. This geranium/pelargonium thing can be confusing, but to keep things clear, I will refer to the bedding and zonal "geraniums" as pelargoniums. Along with zonal geraniums, so-called "ivy geraniums" and "scented geraniums" are pelargoniums as well.

Pelargoniums are native to the Cape of Good Hope in South Africa and reached Holland in 1609. Originally, it was the scented pelargonium that was the attraction. French nurseryman René Morin was growing them in 1621, and English gardener John Tradescant acquired seeds from him in 1631. Britain saw its first pelargonium in 1632, and by the time *P. zonal* was introduced to Britain in 1710, she was all about her brilliant red flowers.

She made it to America in 1760 and evolved quickly from there. Orange-pink, magenta, rose, and scarlet were around by the 1800s, followed by white in 1850. Double-flowered varieties were available in 1864, and by the mid-1850s varieties with tricolored leaves were available.

Pelargonium leaves are medium to coarse in texture; round or lobed; and can be light, medium, dark, and variegated. Red, white, pink, or orange-pink flowers bloom on upright spikes in late spring through early fall. They prefer decently fertile soil in full sun or light shade and moderate watering. The plants will become robust if you feed them well-balanced organic fertilizer every 4 weeks.

Pelargoniums are touted as deer-resistant, but I am skeptical. If deer are anything like my goats (as I assure you they are), then the deer aren't going to even bother trying to resist them.

While many people refer to pelargoniums as annuals, they are actually tender perennials that are *treated* like annuals. If you're especially attached to yours, they can be overwintered and brought indoors by cutting the plant back by a third of its size. Give them a place where they receive bright light (indirect sun) and they will be happy and ready to go back outdoors next spring. Although pelargoniums can be started from seed, that's the long way home and probably not worth the effort. They are incredibly easy to propagate from stem cuttings.

Pelargoniums flower in red, pink, white, and orange-pink late spring through fall.

Take cuttings from a healthy plant that's free of disease and pests. Use a hand pruner or sharp knife and remove a 4- to 6-inch-long cutting from the tip of the stem. Make a straight cut across the stem just below a node (the swollen area on the stem where leaves are attached). If you take cuttings from more than one plant, disinfect your shears after each plant with a solution of equal parts rubbing alcohol and water.

Fill a small container or pot with a blend of potting soil and perlite (pure potting soil is okay too). At this point, you can dip the cutting into a rooting hormone. However, that's not usually necessary for pelargonium cuttings. Remove all the leaves from the bottom half of the cutting (the part that will be buried in the soil).

The soil in the container should be thoroughly wet (not sopping). Plant the cutting about halfway into the container. Water the cutting only when the soil begins to look dry. Don't cover it with plastic, as is done for some other plants. Once they have rooted well, harden the plants off outdoors by allowing them only morning sun for a couple of weeks. Transplant your new pelargonium!

Drink Recipes

Flowers are the next big thing for cocktails, mocktails, lemonades, coffees, teas, smoothies, and hot chocolates. Try these recipes below and see if you don't find yourself coming up with your own floral drinks.

Blue Goddess Smoothie

This smoothie is just begging for an adorable paper straw. You're about to fill up on a power drink fit for a goddess!

INGREDIENTS

1½ cups almond milk

1 frozen banana

1 cup frozen blueberries

1¼ teaspoons lemon zest

1½ teaspoons chia seeds

½ teaspoon dried lavender flowers

¼ teaspoon pure vanilla extract

Add all ingredients to the blender and blend 'er up!

Rose Water and Lemon Sparkler (Cocktail/Mocktail)

This rose and lavender floral cocktail is perfect for a summer garden party. The recipe is easily converted from "cocktail" to "mocktail" by simply leaving out the vodka.

INGREDIENTS

1½ to 2 ounces vodka

1½ tablespoons honey

2 tablespoons rose water

2 tablespoons fresh lemon juice

A smidge of pomegranate juice for lovely color

Ice

¾ cup sparkling water

Fresh roses

Pour the vodka, honey, rose water, lemon juice, and pomegranate juice into a cocktail shaker and fill it with ice. Shake-shake-shake until all ingredients are combined. Pour the mixture into a glass (straining out the ice), and add the sparkling water. Drop a few fresh roses on the top. Each of the ingredients above should be modified according to what pleases your palate.

Lavender-Honey Simple Syrup

Keep some of this syrup on hand to flavor coffee, hot chocolate, cocktails, and mocktails.

INGREDIENTS

1 cup water

1 tablespoon organic lavender flowers

1 cup honey

½ cup sugar

In a saucepan, bring the water and lavender to a boil over medium-high heat. Next, add the honey and the sugar, stirring until they are dissolved. Reduce the heat and let it simmer for 10 minutes. Remove the pan from the heat and let the lavender steep for 20 minutes. Pour the syrup through a mesh strainer into a sterilized glass jar, separating the lavender buds from the syrup. Let it cool and store in the refrigerator for up to 2 weeks.

Create a Victorian Garden Journal

You may already be keeping a garden journal of the flowers you have grown—your favorites, how well they did, and how you can grow them better next year. What you might *not* be doing is making your journal a work of art. Journaling doesn't have to be just about the words on the page. Adding the actual plants, seeds, and drawings will make your journal a thing of beauty. The Victorians were masters at these pressed-flower catalogs. Take yours to a new level.

Start with a three-ring binder as your journal base and add:

- Pressed flowers carefully glued onto a medium-weight paper

- Plastic sleeves that are divided into separate sections (such as business card holders) to house your pressed flowers and dried seeds

- Glassine coin envelopes to hold dried seeds for next season

- Your own plant sketches and drawings

HOW TO FRAME PRESSED FLOWERS

How special is it when the botanical art in your home comes from the flowers in your heirloom garden? Remove flower heads from the plant in the late morning on a dry day. By 11:00 a.m., the dew will have evaporated, yet the afternoon sun will not have had time to wilt the flowers.

MATERIALS

Flowers

Sheets of printer paper

Large, thick book

Heirloom flowers that press well include:

Calendula (*Calendula* spp.)

California poppies (*Eschscholzia californica*)

Chocolate daisy (*Berlandiera lyrata*)

Coreopsis (*Coreopsis* spp.)

Cosmos (*Cosmos bipinnatus*)

Dahlias (*Dahlia* spp.)

Delphiniums (*Delphinium* spp.)

French marigolds (*Tagetes* spp.)

Japanese anemone (*Anemone japonica*)

Johnny-jump-ups (*Viola tricolor*)

Larkspur (*Consolida ajacis*)

Nicotiana (*Nicotiana alata*)

Rose-of-Sharon (*Hibiscus syriacus*)

Zinnias (*Zinnia* spp.)

PRESSING FLOWERS
USING BOOKS

1 Open the first third of a large, thick book. Lay a piece of printer paper on one of the pages and place flowers on the printer page so they are not touching. Flowers with thick centers, such as marigold, dahlia, and zinnia, should have their petals pulled free from the heads before placing them in the book. Don't forget to write the name of the flowers at the bottom of the paper.

2 Place another piece of paper over the flowers you just laid out so that they are now sandwiched between both sheets. Carefully grab the next one-third of the book pages and close it so that the flowers are sandwiched between the printer paper and book pages. Repeat the process using the same book.

3 Keep the pressed flowers evenly weighted by placing more books (or a cinderblock) on top of the pressed flower book. In 2 to 3 weeks, carefully open the book and remove your dried, pressed flowers.

FRAMING YOUR PRESSED FLOWERS

Framing pressed flowers so they become unique art pieces for the home is so simple, you'll want to make several more for gift giving. Have a variety of decorative paper on hand both for gluing the flowers onto, as well as a larger, background sheet that "frames" the art.

MATERIALS

Picture frame

Ruler

Decorative sheets of paper

Scissors

Pressed flowers

Tweezers

White craft glue

Small bowl

Toothpicks

1 Remove the glass from the picture frame.

2 With a ruler, measure the back of the picture frame and make sure that the paper you'd like to use as a background is the same size.

3 If the frame is a different size, use the ruler and the scissors to cut the paper so it fits properly. You can glue the flowers onto this paper or you can use this paper to "frame" a smaller piece of paper that has the glued flowers.

4 If you choose to use a paper that fits the frame, as well as a smaller one that has the flowers, you'll need to cut the one that will have the flowers on it about 1 inch smaller than the larger paper on all sides.

5 Choose the flowers you'll use to create your botanical art piece. You might use various flowers that are all the same color tones. You could choose just two or three flowers, or just one type of flower. You could place the flowers separately or lay them on one another to look like a bouquet.

6 Using the tweezers, arrange them on the paper until you're happy with the design.

7 Squeeze glue from the bottle into the small bowl for easy access.

8 Pick up the flowers with the tweezers and use a toothpick to place a small spot of glue on the back of the flower. Glue the flower onto the paper.

9 After you have finished creating the design, let the glue dry overnight. Then put the frame back together with the flower art inside.

RESOURCES

Get Your Heirlooms Here

Each of these heirloom flower resources is fabulous in its own way. I've listed them here in alphabetical order so you can experience them for yourself and find your own favorites. The wonderful resources listed here are, of course, not exhaustive and are subject to change at any time after this printing.

The Antique Rose Emporium

www.antiqueroseemporium.com
9300 Lueckemeyer Road
Brenham, TX 77833
979.836.9051

Baker Creek Heirloom Seed Co.

www.rareseeds.com
2278 Baker Creek Road
Mansfield, MO 65704
417.924.8917

BBB Seed

www.bbbseed.com
6595 Odell Place, Unit G
Boulder, CO 80301
303.530.1222

Botanical Interests

www.botanicalinterests.com
660 Compton Street
Broomfield, CO 80020
877.821.4340

Bountiful Gardens

www.bountifulgardens.org
1712-D South Main Street
Willits, CA 95490
707.459.6410

The Cottage Gardener

www.cottagegardener.com
4199 Gilmore Road
Newtonville, ON L0A 1J0
905.786.2388

Eden Brothers

www.edenbrothers.com
2099 Brevard Road
Arden, NC 28704
828.633.6338

Heirloom Roses

www.heirloomroses.com/roses
24062 NE Riverside Drive
St. Paul, OR 97137
800.820.0465

Heritage Flower Farm

www.heritageflowerfarm.com
33725 Highway L (Janesville Drive)
Mukwonago, WI 53149
262.662.0804

J. L. Hudson, Seedsman

www.jlhudsonseeds.net
P.O. Box 337
La Honda, CA 94020-0337

Johnny's Selected Seeds

www.johnnyseeds.com
13 Main Street
Fairfield, Maine
877.564.6697

Old House Gardens

www.oldhousegardens.com
4175 Whitmore Lake Road
Ann Arbor, MI 48105
734.995.1486

Peaceful Valley Farm and Garden Supply

www.groworganic.com
125 Clydesdale Court
Grass Valley, CA 95945
530.272.4769

Renee's Garden

www.reneesgarden.com
6060 Graham Hill Road
Felton, CA 95018
888.880.7228

Seed Savers Exchange

www.seedsavers.org
3094 North Winn Road
Decorah, IA 52101
563.382.5990

Select Seeds

www.selectseeds.com
180 Stickney Hill Road
Union, CT 06076
800.684.0395

The Shop at Monticello

www.monticelloshop.org/farm-garden-seeds.html
P.O. Box 318
Charlottesville, VA 22902
800.243.1743

Southern Exposure Seed Company

www.southernexposure.com
P.O. Box 460
Mineral, VA 23117
540.894.9480

Terroir Seeds/Underwood Gardens

www.underwoodgardens.com
P.O. Box 4995
Chino Valley, AZ 86323
888.878.5247

Victory Seed Company

www.victoryseeds.com
P.O. Box 192
Molalla, OR 97038
503.829.3126

Visit Heirloom Flower Gardens

Colonial Williamsburg Foundation – Gardens

www.history.org/history/CWLand/gardensmap.cfm
P.O. Box 1776
Williamsburg, VA 23187
757.229.1000

Garfield Farm Museum

www.garfieldfarm.org
P.O. Box 403
La Fox, IL 60147
630.584.8485

Mount Vernon House and Gardens

www.mountvernon.org
3200 Mount Vernon Memorial
Highway
Mount Vernon, VA 22121
703.780.2000

Old Salem Museum and Gardens

www.oldsalem.org
600 South Main Street
Winston-Salem, NC 27101
336.721.7300

Thomas Jefferson Center for Historic Plants

www.monticello.org/site/house-
and-gardens/thomas-jefferson-
center-historic-plants
P.O. Box 316
Charlottesville, VA 22902
434.984.9800

Good Reads

These heirloom books deserve a
place on your nightstand too.

*A Garden to Dye For: How to
Use Plants from the Garden to
Create Natural Colors for Fabrics
and Fibers* by Chris McLaughlin

*"A Rich Spot of Earth": Thomas
Jefferson's Revolutionary Garden
at Monticello* by Peter J. Hatch

*Beatrix Potter's Gardening Life:
The Plants and Places That
Inspired the Classic Children's
Tales* by Marta McDowell

*Floret Farm's Cut Flower Garden:
Grow, Harvest, and Arrange
Stunning Seasonal Blooms* by Erin
Benzakein and Julie Chai

*Gardening with Heirloom
Seeds: Tried-and-True Flowers,
Fruits, and Vegetables for a New
Generation* by Lynn Coulter

*Gertrude Jekyll and the Country
House Garden: From the
Archives of Country Life* by
Judith B. Tankard

*Heirloom Flowers: Vintage
Flowers for Modern Gardens*
by Tovah Martin

Monet's Garden at Giverny
by Jean-Pierre Gilson

*Of Naked Ladies and Forget-Me-
Nots: The Stories Behind
the Common Names of Some
of Our Favorite Plants* by
Allan M. Armitage

Passalong Plants by Steve
Bender and Felder Rushing
Tasha Tudor's Garden by
Tovah Martin and Richard
W. Brown

Other Goodies

American Herbalists Guild

www.americanherbalistsguild.com

Authentic Haven Brand Natural Brew

Authentic Haven Brand
Natural Brew makes it easy to
feed your flowers and plants
100-percent naturally. Haven
Brand uses the highest quality
cow and horse manures from
livestock raised on native pastures
at the Haven Family Ranch.

Packaged in an environmentally
friendly tea bag, simply drop a
"moo poo" tea bag into a 5-gallon
bucket of water steep for a few
days. Then you have an organic,
nutrient-rich fertilizer tea for
your heirlooms!
www.manuretea.com
949.248.1249

Dharma Trading Company

This is where I get the silk scarves
that I use in my botanical dyes.
There is all kinds of dyeing
goodness going on at Dharma.
Prices are great too.
www.dharmatrading.com
800.542.5227

Santa Clarita Valley Rose Society

These rosarians have great
information on old garden,
antique, and heirloom roses.
www.santaclaritarose.org

Three Angry Kids Soaps

Did you check out those cool
artisan soaps in Chapter 3?
Snag some for yourself right here.
www.threeangrykids.com
530.903.8129

University of Maryland Medical Center – Herbal Medicine

www.umm.edu/health/medical/
altmed/treatment/herbal-medicine

ABOUT THE AUTHOR

Chris McLaughlin is a Northern California writer and author who has had her hands in the soil for nearly forty years. She's the author of seven books, including *A Garden to Dye For* (St. Lynn's Press) and *Vertical Vegetable Gardening* (Alpha Books).

Chris's work can be found in *Hobby Farm Home Magazine*, *Urban Farm* magazine, *Heirloom Gardener* magazine, *Mother Earth Living*, and *Fine Gardening* magazine. Online, she's written for a variety of gardening sites, including VegetableGardener.com, About.com, Fix.com, and *From Scratch* magazine.

Chris and her family live on a flower and fiber farm in the Northern California foothills, where they grow flowers, fruit, and vegetables and raise Angora goats. Feel free to hunt her down at *Flowers Ink* (www.flowersink.com).

DEDICATION

For my husband and plant partner, Bobby,
who lives with a ghost when it's book-writing time.

(Seriously, you're becoming a mighty fine cook.)

ACKNOWLEDGMENTS

This is the place where I get to thank my people. I am thrilled to be a part of the Cool Springs Press/Quarto family. A huge hug and thank-you to Shawna Coronado for introducing me to her editor and for her creative wisdom. Thank you to my fabulous editors, Mark Johanson, Madeleine Vasaly, Alyssa Bluhm, and Karen Levy, for allowing me the creative freedom of the heirloom flowers topic. An extra-big squeeze to Bryan Trandem for getting me and my vision.

To my youngest daughter, Bella: I couldn't think of a more beautiful model for the heirloom flower crown. Artistic photographer Nadeen Flynn shot the majority of the gorgeous photos for this book. Thank you for taking on this project, and I hope you enjoyed it as much as I did. A heartfelt thank-you to the inspiring Tovah Martin, who has fallen for the same lovely things that are dear to my heart. Melissa at Flowers on Main Florist for coming to my rescue; Kate at Dancing Beetle Flower Farm and Cyndee at Cyndee's Flowers for letting us shoot at your farms and for your friendship;

Diane Estrada at Three Angry Kids for your soap artistry. Penny Tank Brown for her unwavering encouragement. Big, smooshing hugs to Jenny Peterson, who just keeps on answering that phone, poor thing. Big love to Deanne Gossler, who now knows more about heirloom flowers than she ever wanted to know. Side winks to Bob and Hunter McLaughlin, my in-house editors.

I am greatly indebted to these people who not only inspire me, but contributed to this book in their unique ways. While there are only one or two names on the cover, I assure you that this is an illusion. Help from my husband, kids, grandkids, friends, editors, flower farmers, florists with flower hunting, panic, photo shoots, DIYing, insane writing hours, and a farm contributed to the first draft of this book. Weeks later, when the big edits showed up, the raw manuscript was a symphony of fonts, colors, and notes. Questions were addressed and additions incorporated, and the book became much more than it ever could have been, as it's a collaboration of many creative hands.

Thank you all for letting me have my name on the cover.

INDEX

PHOTO CREDITS